What is success? Many people today commit their lives to pursue wealth, power, prestige, material possessions, and prosperity. All too often, when their hopes and dreams are dashed upon the rocks of reality, their faith in God is shattered, their self-esteem crumbles, and they become disillusioned with life. They have mistakenly believed that God promises material success to all His children if they try to attain it hard enough. In The Success Factor, *Dr. Archibald D. Hart presents a realistic view of the abundant life proclaimed in the Gospel. He discusses how to make your success in life in accord with your God-given potential. Dr. Hart introduces you to* reality thinking–*"a way of thinking realistically about yourself, the world in which you live, the God in Whom you believe, and His purpose for your life." By thinking sensibly and logically–and acknowledging God's control in your life–you can learn to master your thoughts and enjoy a life filled with: love…joy …optimism…confidence…serenity…poise…faith…courage …cheerfulness…imagination…initiative…tolerance…honesty …humility…enthusiasm–all* true *blessings from God.* The Success Factor *will help you discover God's wonderful plan for you and show you how to pursue it.*

D0878976

BY Archibald D. Hart
Feeling Free

The Success Factor

Archibald D. Hart

Fleming H. Revell Company
Old Tappan, New Jersey

Unless otherwise identified, Scripture quotations are based on the King James Version of the Bible.

Scripture quotations identified NEB are from the New English Bible. © The Delegates of the Oxford University Press and the Syndics of the Cambridge University Press 1961 and 1970. Reprinted by permission.

Scripture quotations identified RSV are from the Revised Standard Version of the Bible, copyrighted 1946, 1952, © 1971 and 1973.

Scripture quotations identified TLB are from The Living Bible, copyright © 1971 by Tyndale House Publishers, Wheaton, IL. Used by permission.

Library of Congress Cataloging in Publication Data
Hart, Archibald D.
    The success factor.
    "Power books"—Cover.
    Includes bibliographical references.
    1. Success.   2. Christian life—1960-   . I. Title.
BJ1611.2.H32   1984   248.4   83-23065
ISBN 0-8007-5138-8 (pbk.)

Acknowledgments

There are several people who have helped me develop the ideas for this book and bring it to completion:

- My life partner and mother of my three beautiful daughters, Kathleen, whose patience and willingness to help with the most menial of chores was always an inspiration. She has researched for me, loved me, and supported every endeavor I have ever undertaken.
- My professional colleague and partner, Dr. Paul Peterson, who together with my psychological assistants, Jim Childerston, Richard Blackmon, and Carol Heukrodt, were always ready to serve as sounding boards and interact with my ideas.
- Fritz Ridenour, whose confidence in and pursuit of my ideas brought this book into existence.
- My secretary, Darylene Hansen, who typed, typed, and retyped, with constant enthusiasm and encouragement.
- My patients, too numerous to mention, from whom I have learned so much and who have helped me to grow and become the person I believe God wants me to be.

To all of you I say—thank you! I dedicate this book to each and every one of you. You are all deeply loved.

Contents

Preface

We all want to be successful. Every patient I have ever worked with, every friend I have known, and every colleague I have ever been associated with wants to be successful. Deeply spiritual ministers want to be successful. They want to feel that the hours they spend toiling in preaching and pastoring will bring abundant rewards for the Kingdom of God. No one wants to feel that his or her life has been wasted.

Is there anything wrong with this? I think not, except that two questions arising from our modern preoccupation with success bother me. First, *How* does one achieve success? Second, *What* is success, anyway? These questions are the concern of this book.

When I stop someone and ask, "What does success mean to you?" I get some varied and strange answers. There seems to be no universal agreement on what it is. The truth is that while we all want to be successful, few of us have clearly defined what it means for ourselves. When I ask, "How does one achieve success?" I get responses like "You've got to believe in yourself" or "You've got to think positively and believe that anything is possible." In fact, there pervades nearly all branches of the Christian church today a "gospel of success" that competes very strongly with the true Gospel in the amount of attention it gets. It is a gospel that says, "God wills your prosperity," notwithstanding the conditions of discipleship. It is clearly a false gospel that could easily lead to the downfall of many because its central focus is on the material and not the spiritual.

9

To the Christian the quest for success in certain areas can be hazardous. The pitfalls are many and the temptations to sin, subtle. In our culture so much emphasis is placed on material things that it is easy to think of success only in terms of money, possessions, power, or prestige. But is this all there is to success? Should the search for achievement be confined to them? Should not the Christian also think of being successful in those qualities of human existence that have eternal value? It seems to me that we can *only* satisfy our deep need for fulfillment by being successful in honesty, charity, patience, spirituality, and the development of desirable personality characteristics.

Is success open to everyone? Can a housewife and mother pursue success with all the enthusiasm of a business entrepreneur? Can a retired bank clerk or missionary still pursue successfulness? They certainly can, if they carefully define what success means to them.

Do I believe it is important to be successful in work, business, or professional endeavors? I certainly do. But too many of us have been taught to seek success only in these realms. Our priorities have thus become distorted. We have neglected the other, more important, aspects of life. We have become lopsided and unbalanced, and this has robbed us of poise and peace. We pay the penalty for this in increased stress, depression, and misery.

I would like to call us back to a balanced understanding of what it means to be successful. I have coined the term *holistic success* to describe the view that true success must embrace *all* of life—spiritual, physical, and psychological—if it is to be a Christianly creative and healing force out of which happiness will come. By *holistic* I simply mean "whole, complete, sound, and free from flaws." I also mean that it is "holy" in the sense that God will bless it because it will bring us closer to Him. It is the embodiment of all God wills for our lives. It is the integration of every aspect of our being into a cohesive and spiritual whole. It is a success that is pure and unblemished, undivided, unbroken, and completely healthy.

Am I being a little idealistic? I hope not, because I sincerely believe that we need to restore the priority of eternity over the "here and now" in all our thinking and questing.

I see holistic success as a falling in love with life, especially the life we can live in Christ. I see it as a life full of love, joy, optimism, confidence, serenity, poise, faith, courage, cheerfulness, imagination, initiative, tolerance, honesty, humility, and enthusiasm.

How does one become successful? Modern-day preachers tell us that we must think "positively," or that we must become "possibility thinkers." They try to convince us that we can create our own success whenever we want to because it is all around us. I don't disagree with these sentiments. I just believe that there is a little more to the "secret" than this. My central concern is that we do not distort reality in our search for success.

To achieve holistic success I am presenting a way of thinking that counters much of our present-day emphasis on unreality.

Many would have us believe that this is the age of mind-miracles. We are told that our minds can perform the most remarkable feats. The reason we are not making millions of dollars or experiencing the most fantastic ecstasy is that our minds are too restricted. We have been taught that we think too negatively and that we set our sights too low. We do not "believe" in ourselves and the tremendous possibilities within us.

Is this the *success factor?* I don't believe so. For one, I don't think it is biblical. The idea that self-reliance is sufficient and that *all* a person needs to be successful lies within him or herself is erroneous and misleading. I prefer to believe that God came to save us from our self-sufficiency, no matter how brilliant or competent we may be. We need God, whether we acknowledge it or not.

It is true that many of us have problems in our thinking, and this makes us quite gullible to the merchants of success techniques. We so desperately want to be successful that we grasp at any gimmick or idea that would make it possible. We are easily seduced from reality. We jump at "positive," or other forms of thinking, in the hope that it will give us what we are seeking.

In this book I call us back to *reality thinking* as the critical factor in all success. This is simply a way of being honest at *all* levels of thought life. As you will see, it is a way of thinking realistically about ourselves, the world in which we live, the God in whom we believe, and His purpose for our lives.

I have divided the book into three parts. Each has its own purpose and should be read as a whole.

If you feel like a total failure, this book is for you. If you are confused and fear that you will never become a fully functioning person, I think this book can help you. If your emotions control you instead of your controlling them, then reality thinking is for you. If you are stuck in a meaningless rut of family and work drudgery, take hope. All is not lost. There is a glorious and meaningful purpose for your life, if you will have the faith to pursue it. Remember these words of Paul:

> And he said unto me, My grace is sufficient for thee: for my strength is made perfect in weakness. Most gladly therefore will I rather glory in my infirmities, that the power of Christ may rest upon me.
> 2 Corinthians 12:9.

DR. ARCHIBALD D. HART
PASADENA, CALIFORNIA

PART ONE
A Realistic Approach to Success

Part one comprises four chapters. In chapter 1 I examine the whole matter of our preoccupation with being successful and try to broaden our understanding of what it means to be successful as a Christian. I suggest that we must be successful in *all* aspects of our being. In chapter 2 I emphasize the importance of *reality thinking* as the way to discover God's potential for your life and for creating a healthy personality and spirituality. In chapter 3 I continue to develop the importance of reality thinking and show how it encompasses positive and other forms of thinking. Finally, in chapter 4 I stress the fact that each of us has limits, and we must find these as well as discover our "gifts" if we are going to be balanced, healthy, and holistically successful.

It is my prayer that you will come to love reality. We are all consummate dreamers. We love turning every incident, experience, encounter, and relationship into a fantasy of wants, musts, oughts, and shoulds. Truth about our world is better. Fantasy doesn't exist. Reality brings out the best in creativity from us. Come with me as we learn how to better understand and deal with it.

What Does God Think of Success?

Everyone wonders, at times, whether life has any meaning. I do, and I am sure you do also. The young child bewildered by the complexities of life; the teenager overcome by powerful urges that both excite and disquiet him; the young mother struggling to keep her cool while the baby screams; the single adult disillusioned with relationships; the grandfather about to retire from his job of forty years. They all, at times, ask, "What does life have to offer me?"

It is natural to want the most out of life.

I clearly remember when I was about twelve years of age, retreating with five or six of my closest buddies to our favorite gang hideout and talking about the future by the light of two candles and a small wood fire. We talked for many hours of great fame, fantasized great accomplishments, and dreamed of distant travels. Even at this early age we had a sense of the importance of squeezing the fruit of life to the last drop. We wanted our lives to count for something, especially since none of us came from wealthy homes or felt that we had been given any special start in life. We were just an ordinary bunch of kids who wanted to live life to the fullest.

Recently I had occasion to review some of my early life dreams. I was pleasantly surprised to discover that I had fulfilled almost every one of them. I had set my goals realistically and followed my quest with the gusto of a Don Quixote, and with God's help I am doing what He wants me to do. That's not true of all my childhood buddies. Only one, at the most, has "made it" in terms of worldly achievement, but in the final analysis their happiness will be determined by many other factors. And that's what this book is about.

What Are Your Life Goals?

Before we proceed any further, why not take a sheet of paper and make a list of five goals you have had for your life. Go back in time as far as you can remember and recapture your life dreams. Then write down five reasons why you believe you have not or cannot achieve some or all of these goals. Keep these answers close by you as you continue to read.

For many, meaning in life comes fundamentally from being successful: successful in business, in finances, in climbing the ladder of promotion, in love, in relationships, in child rearing, and in having fun. Without success in some of these areas, life has no meaning, happiness, or contentment. But this is not the end of the matter.

How Much Success Is Enough?

We all realize that *some* success is necessary for a happy, satisfying life, but how much success is enough? In how many areas of life must one be successful to feel satisfied? If you have a happy marriage, should you also be successful in business? If you are an effective parent, should you also be successful in your business investments? If you are a powerful and life-changing preacher, should you also be a master of administration? If you are a brilliant surgeon, should you be a master gardener also? This is where the drive for success so valued in our culture can get out of hand. Instead of its bringing a deep sense of satisfaction, some success breeds a desire for more success in the big issues of life. Much unhappiness, therefore, is caused by our not being content to be successful in lesser areas. If we only want to be successful in the major areas of life, we are bound to create unhappiness. If we pursue it in *all* of life, with a balance between the big and the little, we have a greater chance of being deeply happy.

Myths About Success

We have been conned by current trends in our culture into believing a number of myths about success. One myth is that unless we are constantly seeking and achieving success in wealth, possessions, pleasure, health, and self-fulfillment, we cannot be happy. If we are not reaching for the stars and thinking that *all* is possible, we are missing some great purpose for our lives. While I want to show how you can be more successful in the important areas of your life, including your personal walk with God, I do not want to create the idea that you *must* be constantly seeking a high degree of success in everything you want to do. This is unrealistic. You will wear yourself out. Clarify what it is you want out of life and what it is you believe God wants to give you. Then be content to seek the fulfillment of this dream.

Another myth is that only money and possessions are the real prizes of life. Many people feel they have failed because they have not been able to accumulate a certain amount of wealth. Our materialistic culture teaches us to derive our sense of achievement from a fat bank balance and a long list of investments. We give more value to this than to being successful in controlling our tempers, demonstrating the love of Christ to others, or achieving a deep sense of abiding inner peace. Consequently, we can easily become miserable and feel unfulfilled even when we have "much goods laid up for many years" (Luke

12:19). A third myth is that we can only be happy when we have accomplished a goal we have personally set and pursued for ourselves. We are encouraged to "be our own person and find our own dream."

While the success of achieving a goal can be very satisfying, if you are a Christian it can only be a *lasting* satisfaction if it also fulfills God's purpose for your life. I cannot stress this point too strongly. To achieve great success doing what is outside of God's will for you, *cannot* bring deep abiding joy. It only provides a flash in the pan! Success must mesh with God's plan for your life. If this sounds like a cliché, I'm sorry, but I believe it is true. In fact, your innermost being will crave this fulfillment of God's plan. You will not be at peace until you find it. This may mean that you cannot do what *you* want to do, but is doing what you want to do really that important, anyway?

Perhaps the most damaging myth of all is the one so prevalent in Christian circles. It says that if you are willing to accept the responsibilities that come with being successful, God will lead you into success of any sort. Mostly, this myth relates to wealth and is built on the idea that since God created everything (including all the gold), He is free to give it to whomever He wants. But it's not this simple. I doubt if there would be enough gold to go around for all earthly ages. True, God wills our prosperity. For a few it may be wealth. For most of us the prosperity we should seek is what we really desperately need: godliness and contentment. "For we brought nothing into this world, and it is certain we can carry nothing out" (1 Timothy 6:7).

The Disillusionment of Material Success

Many have worked frantically in their quest for success. They have toiled for long hours, used all the positive-thinking principles they could muster, suffered many deprivations, and finally accomplished their dreams. They have achieved SUCCESS . . . only to discover that it isn't what they thought it would be. Instead of a pot of gold at the end of the rainbow, they have found a bucket of misery. Are you surprised? I'm not!

Take Gary, for example. We grew up together. He knew he was going to be successful from the time he was a teenager. His parents were wealthy, so I envied his start in life. He lived around successful people and could absorb their "ambience." He enjoyed the thrill of a business gamble and, especially, the ecstatic pleasure of achieving a goal or accomplishing a deal to his advantage, as many of us experienced even during our high-school years. Then we went our different ways and I lost touch with him.

Occasionally I heard of his achievements. Success did not come easily or suddenly to Gary. That only happens in fairy stories. In real life, success takes lots of hard work, and there are often many setbacks. But Gary had what it took to be successful. He was persistent. He could persevere.

When I met him again twenty years later, he looked like an old man. He had a flashy automobile but an unhappy face. He was miserable even though he could buy anything he wanted or go anywhere he pleased. He was crabby and suspicious and a pain to relate to. Most important of all, while in his youth he professed to be a Christian, he was further from God now than I could have imagined.

What had all this material success brought him? Nothing that counted in this life and certainly nothing that would count in eternity. If anything, his success had robbed him of the only opportunity given him to live a really meaningful life. He had wasted it trying to be successful in business, and he had nothing but money to show for it.

But this is not to say that success cannot ever be joyous. Of course it can! I know many very successful people. Quite a few are successful in both their business and personal lives. Many are happy and contented. But I doubt whether *any* of them would say that their happiness comes just from their business successes. I believe these people would be happy *even* if they were *not* successful in material things. And herein lies the secret of true happiness. It is because they are capable of finding happiness in rags that they can find it in their riches. Ponder this thought, because it is very true. It does *not* work the other way around!

This, then, is a very important ground rule for all Christians seeking success of any sort: *You won't find happiness in worldly success unless you can create it without such success.*

The Hazards of Success

Even when we sincerely seek God's will for our lives, there are hazards to be negotiated in the pursuit of success. This is especially true in the realm of material things. If you are seeking success in business, your career, investments, or simply in power and prestige, here are some very important points which you should consider carefully and prayerfully:

• Don't make the achieving of success the only basis for your happiness in life. Seek happiness in your faith and in your personal walk with God. Then you will be able to weather the struggles and disappointments of your quest.

• Be careful not to define success only in terms of money, promotion, prestige, power, or possessions. Seek after the fruits of God's spirit. Value above all else the development of a Christlike spirit.

• Know when enough success is enough. Too many are trapped by an ever-accelerating merry-go-round of success. They just don't know when to get off.

• Avoid the sense of omnipotence that success brings. It is delusional to think that only you can do something. Be willing to delegate to others. You are dispensable in God's plan. Treat it as a great privilege to be a part of it.

• Know your limits. Learn the signs of exhaustion and burnout and be courageous in seeking healing if you must. Most successful people ultimately succumb to the ravages of stress. The achievement of success has been negated by the destruction that stress has caused in their bodies.

• Constantly work at understanding and changing your

values. Know yourself and why you want things. Be clear about the preeminence of eternal matters over the present. Rust and moth will corrupt all you can touch, see, and feel. Invest in eternity for the best rewards.

• Keep God in your success. Few people really know how to cope with success once it is attained and slowly inch God out. Only God can keep us balanced, free of inflated egos, and humble in our achievements.

Only One Life

In the consideration of what God thinks of success there is one last point to be made before I expand on the idea of holistic success. It is this: We only get *one* turn at living.

Do you grasp this? There are *no* second chances. Either we get it right the first time or we lose in the game of life. God has planned it this way. No rehearsals. No dry runs. This means that we have a responsibility to plan and live our lives in such a way that we achieve the full potential of what God wants us to be. The soonest we can do this is now. Yesterday is gone. Tomorrow is too late.

Usually the truth that there is only one life to live does not bother us too much when we are young, because we believe that there is still plenty of time to "do our thing." But when we reach our forties and fifties the realization that life has a finite limit begins to awaken in us. This awakening can strike like a tornado and wreak havoc in a life. When it does, we call it a mid-life crisis and it often sends men scampering for a second try at romance and fortune. After the sixties it can be the cause of serious depression.

I believe I was fortunate in that the full impact of life's shortness dawned on me in my mid-twenties. I don't recall all the circumstances, but I remember that when I was quite young, my grandmother would often say to me, "Archie, life is very short, so don't waste your minutes and you won't waste your life." She taught me to value each day and live it to the full. She always viewed a day in which she was angry with someone as a wasted day and would determine not to repeat it.

These ideas must have impacted me greatly because I have lived a full life, learned many enjoyable skills, and know how to experience the richness of living. My grandmother was also a very godly woman. She taught me the truth that "the only thing that really counts is finding and fulfilling God's purpose for your life." Nothing else matters! But at the same time everything else falls into its rightful place. I have never doubted that these words of Romans 8:28 are true:

> And we know that all things work together for good to them that love God, to them who are the called according to his purpose.

Are you at the stage of life where you feel handicapped or even paralyzed by the realization that life is passing you by and that you will not be able to live out your life dream? Perhaps you feel like a total failure in your business or marriage. Perhaps you are a minister who is disillusioned with your ministry and angry at people for not being responsive to God's calling. Maybe you were recently widowed and must face the rest of life all alone. Whatever your life circumstance, and no matter where you are in your journey, you are never beyond the possibility of success in the way God sees it.

You may have wasted your life this far, but do you have to continue wasting it? Whether you have fifty years still to live, or only fifty hours, the balance of your life must be lived out in harmony with God's will. If you do this you are SUCCESSFUL in the holistic sense I have described in the preface. You are integrating every opportunity available to you with every ounce of potential within you.

Don't waste your time regretting the past. This can destroy your future. When my wife and I were first married, we lived in South Africa next to an elderly Christian couple, in the same apartment building. We came to love this couple even though they were almost fifty years older than we were. We had candlelight dinners together, enjoyed listening to music together, prayed and sang hymns together. We soon forgot our age differences as we became very close.

But there was one dark cloud over our friendship. This wonderful couple, over seventy years of age, spent most of their waking hours talking and complaining about how they had not made a success of their life. They regretted not having served their Lord in some full-time capacity. They had "wasted" their life, they felt, in humdrum routine and an ordinary existence. They believed their usefulness was over and behaved accordingly.

In prayer together one evening, I felt I should challenge this perpetual looking back. "Uncle Bill," I said, "have you ever thought that no matter how you have wasted your life to this point, God still has a way in which you can feel useful and successful, whether you only live one more year or ten?" Both he and his lovely, old wife thought. They began to ask themselves, "Is life really over at seventy? Isn't there something useful God can do with us?" Very soon they heard that a mission hospital in a primitive part of the country needed a handyman to do routine building maintenance. Uncle Bill was a master handyman!

To condense the story, they served twelve beautiful years performing a most valuable service to a needy people. Uncle Bill's wife was an artist. She became the illustrator for a series of Christian African children's stories that are masterpieces.

This is what holistic success is all about. It is believing that you must make the best use of every minute of life. It is too precious to waste in pursuing the wrong goals for success or spending time regretting what could have been.

A Holistic View of Success

Since this book is about a holistic understanding of success and the type of thinking that can lead to it, it is important that we begin at the right place. As Christians, our chief aim and duty in life is singular and simple: to love God and enjoy Him forever.

Ultimately, success must be measured solely by the degree to which we achieve this aim.

The secular notion of success is that one should constantly be reaching for some new materialistic goal. One psychiatrist put it this way, "After all, there are no reasons to be alive other than the ones you make for yourself." Is it any surprise, therefore, when prominent show-business people say that they have seen it all, that there is nothing else to live for, and then seek relief from "the great boredom" of this life by killing themselves? Not at all. If this is all there is to life, then why bother to live?

But there *is* more to life than novel experiences and the pursuit of social goals, and it is *more* important to be successful in one's personal and spiritual life than in the material. The achievement of success in personal matters is well within the grasp of *all* of us. We can all be better people in the name of Christ. In this book I will try to emphasize this holistic view of success. It puts success within the reach of all of us, from gutter sweepers to brain surgeons; from retired nobodies to business tycoons at the pinnacle of their career. It is, I believe, more consistent and harmonious with the Christian life than any other emphasis.

We need to value being successful in parenting, loving, serving, being patient, caring for others, and controlling our tempers. Success in these areas can be much more deeply satisfying and give real meaning to life because they encompass the more basic functions of life. They are not confined to the physical, but embrace the spiritual and psychological as well. *Success here is making the best of your total self.* In this sense it is *holistic success.* It is both whole and holy.

How does one achieve this holistic success? By many means. I will emphasize that central to most of our success in psychological and spiritual well-being is the way we *think.* Holistic success is the product of the right way of thinking. It is learning to think in the way of God.

Where then is this leading us? Simply to this: Thoughts are powerful determiners of who you are; you don't have to be destroyed by them. You can control and find in them a great reservoir of unused power—for your spiritual, psychological, and physical well-being. You can better serve your Lord in all the realms of your being and follow His purposes with clarity and determination if you will watch, control, and reconstruct your thinking.

I call this approach to the way we should think *reality thinking.* It is a commonsense way of structuring thoughts and tapping the resources of our wonderful Gospel. Thoughts, after all, are only tools. They are not a power in themselves. But they are tools we must learn to use wisely.

Examine again the five reasons why you believe you cannot achieve your goals, as you wrote them down at the beginning of this chapter. How many of them have to do with your thinking or aspects of your beliefs, attitudes, or expectations? If you changed your thinking, would some of these obstacles fall away?

Come with me as we examine, in the next chapter, why reality thinking is the key to success. I will help you to sharpen the tools of your thoughts so that they may be the means of a deeper and more fulfilling life in Christ. To be able to think clearly and nondestructively is a mark of a fully mature Christian. More than this, I would say it is a necessity! Success in all the important aspects of living depends on it. Control over otherwise destructive emotions is achieved by it. And above all, through it we fulfill God's perfect intentions for us because "God hath not given us the spirit of fear, but of power, and of love, and of a *sound* mind" (2 Timothy 1:7, italics added).

Why Reality Thinking Is the Key to Holistic Success

Chapter 2

At thirty-two years of age, Julie has had it with life! She is convinced that there is no God, no hope, and no prospect of a happy and fulfilling existence on this earth. During her first therapy session with me she spoke of lost dreams, abandoned relationships, and lonely nights.

Her present state of mind began three years ago. She was employed by a large organization as a sales manager. Through her own diligence and hard work she had risen the ladder of promotion, past others older than she, and was now competing very effectively in a field traditionally dominated by men.

At first she found her work satisfying. It occupied most of her waking mind, but it fulfilled her. She had done some dating but thought she still had plenty of time ahead of her to settle her matrimonial needs.

Then things began to go wrong. She became restless and unhappy. The seeds of discontentment had been sown. What was once a beautiful garden now began to grow weeds. Beauty gave way to ugliness.

It all started when she read a well-known book on how to improve your life situation. "Health, wealth, and success belongs to everyone," the book said. "Whatever and whoever you are, you can be better," the book encouraged. God wants everyone to be wealthy and successful, and if you serve Him and think His thoughts, success can be yours also!

Julie became obsessed with the idea that she wasn't successful and that she deserved a better deal from life. The only reason she was not the president of her company was that she had not set her goals high enough. This is what she told herself over and over again. She had settled for the clouds when the stars were her destiny. She resigned her position as sales manager and set out to conquer the world of prosperity. Six months later she was deeply depressed. She was not able to find another job. When I first encountered her, she remained isolated in her apartment, withdrawn from all social contacts, brooding through each day, dejected, defeated, and distraught.

Julie had made one fundamental theological error: She believed that it was God's will that everyone should be financially prosperous and personally successful by the standards of this world. Because she believed this, she behaved accordingly—such is the power of beliefs. Her belief is a distortion of God's purposes for His Children. While we are called to live an "abundant life," this abundance has more to do with eternal issues than with what the world sees as prosperity.

Our Dilemma

Julie is not alone in her quest for success and prosperity. We are all caught up in it. We want to be rich and famous—at least those of us who are normal do!

Let me make clear that I am not saying that a search for material abundance has no place in the Christian's life. God can use money, and He certainly uses those who make money to further His Kingdom.

I am also not saying that to think big thoughts, to plan great plans, and to dream impossible dreams has no purpose. It certainly does! Those who think little thoughts only accomplish little deeds. Those who aim low, shoot low.

The truth is that by a variety of means most of us are taught by our culture to underestimate our potential and to be under-achievers. Those who would have us think big and become "possibility" and "positive" thinkers are correct. We are inhibited by puny thoughts and pesky feelings of insecurity. We need to stretch ourselves, set higher goals, and *believe* in ourselves and in the God who has created and saved us. This will maximize the possibility that we will accomplish great things. But! Is there not a danger that we can get caught up in a worldly delusion that makes us believe that God is only on our side when the dollars are rolling in or the honors are flowing strong, and that He has abandoned us when they are not? *Whatever happened to the idea that the surest sign God was with you was that you had a deep abiding peace in your heart?* Where is the truth that God hasn't called us to be successful but obedient?

Human goals and personal ambitions do have their place in the life of the Christian. I know, because I have sought to become all I was meant to be by setting goals for myself and developing my skills to the maximum! I started my working career as an engineer but later switched to clinical psychology because I believed my gifts could be better expressed in this calling. Throughout I have tried to sanctify my ambitions and keep my goals in touch with God's reality. What is God's reality? It is *His perfect plan for my life!* I believe that without these two safeguards the cult of prosperity, so prevalent in evangelical Christianity, is fraught with treacherous pitfalls. The "success syndrome" can cause our downfall.

Success and Your Thoughts

Is there such a thing as strength derived from the right way of thinking? Should a Christian engage in such thinking? Is it true that the average person barely taps 10 percent of their potential to become whatever they want to become? Is it possible to live an entire life and not fulfill the plan God has for you? The answers are yes, yes, yes, and yes.

The simple truth is that you are probably only a fraction of what you can become because you are, like the rest of us, limiting and inhibiting yourself by the way you think. Your thoughts are either your greatest ally or your greatest enemy. They can open you to or shut you off from a great reservoir of unused power, both within yourself and in God. They can unleash your innermost being or imprison you in cages of fear and anxiety.

Thoughts can create feelings of inadequacy and inferiority, or ideas of failure and embarrassment. If you are miserable, unhappy, unfulfilled, incomplete, inhibited, and unspiritual, it is most likely because you engage in a certain style of thinking. Whether you accept it or not, you are the product of a very simple law, stated thousands of years ago by Solomon: "For as he thinketh in his heart, so is he" (Proverbs 23:7).

Your thoughts can either open to you or shut you off from every resource, power, strength, and potential of divine power God has given you. You can enhance or inhibit your personality, foster or stunt your creativity, encourage or discourage your spontaneity and individuality, all by the way you think. In essence, I am saying that your thinking is central to everything you are or can be.

While you don't deliberately choose to be miserable, the fact is that you create an abundance of it by your fearful, unsure, wavering, hesitating, doubting, skeptical, pessimistic, mistrusting, and suspicious thoughts.

You can't love in a free, uninhibited, nurturing, and joyful way when thoughts of rejection, low self-esteem, unworthiness, insecurity, aloneness, and self-hate dog your waking moments and sabotage your personal goals.

Like a polluted stream, your thoughts may flow through your mind defiling every part of your being, corrupting what little purity you have, and soiling the germ of righteousness and longing after holiness planted by God's Spirit.

Let me summarize what I am saying: *Your thoughts may be your downfall.*

They are the poisons that destroy you and the cancers that erode you. They make you or break you. They allow you to become what God wants you to be or they thwart that plan.

Reality Thinking

The purpose I have set myself is to embody the ideas of positive and possibility thinking, which I hold to be liberating, with the truths of reality and the emphasis that cognitive therapy has recently given us, to form a more constructive and biblically sound way of thinking I call *reality thinking.* Reality thinking is different from positive and possibility thinking. While it encourages individuals to attain their full potential by shedding the shackles of their constricted minds and freeing themselves from negative patterns of thinking that are self-destructive and self-limiting, it stresses that *all* thinking must be based on *reality* and that thinking must be sensible and logical.

There is a great risk that people who are taught to think only in terms of positive ideas may distort reality. And there are two main realities to be reckoned with: the reality of life and the reality of God.

The Background to This Book

Let me state that I have the highest regard for the Christian leaders who have focused on the ways of thinking as the key to success. Dr. Norman Vincent Peale, whose ideas about "positive thinking" have permeated much of Western Christendom, has brought health, freedom, and happiness to countless people. His more recent emphasis on the use of "dynamic imaging" is helpful and remarkably close to where much modern psychotherapy is heading. The power of the mind to influence its destiny through self-focus and visualization is only now being recognized as a powerful healing technique. The years ahead will probably see a dramatic revolution in the use of these techniques as a preventive in medicine and psychological health.

Dr. Robert Schuller has expanded Dr. Peale's ideas into what he calls "possibility thinking." In a practical and easy-to-follow way, he has helped many to remove the chains of self-doubt, self-hate, and self-defeat and to move ahead in their lives by encouraging them to use their imagination and *believe* that anything is possible. I am a cognitive psychotherapist, which means that I focus on how the mind thinks, so I appreciate very much the power of beliefs to determine our destiny. Dr. Schuller has put into practice many of the techniques that are only now becoming obvious to psychotherapists. He has, of course, tied possibility thinking to God, the source of all power.

New Dimensions to Positive Thinking?

Both Dr. Peale's and Dr. Schuller's ideas have been revolutionary and liberating. Countless numbers of people can tell stories of healed minds, recovered self-esteem, salvaged families, restored relationships, businesses brought back to life, and career disasters averted because they have followed these principles. No sensible person can deny the value of thinking positively, avoiding negative patterns of self-defeat, and dreaming that the impossible is possible. These thought patterns free us from the prisons of self-defeat, shape our attitudes, and thus our destinies of success or failure.

But many thinking Christians ask the question "Are these ideas truly biblical?" Or, to put it another way, "If we adopt these liberating ideas how can we be sure that we are operating within the limits of biblical truth? How can I be sure that God is in my plans and that my dreams are His dreams?" They wonder about the many who have not become successful and who now are even more disillusioned because their hopes were raised only to be dashed by the reality of life's limitations.

These are the questions I will seek to address. Many evangelical Christians have intuitively felt afraid of positive thinking. They often interpret it as an emphasis on some mysterious "inner force" released by the mind. They have always been suspicious of easy solutions to complex and deep-rooted fundamental human problems. And rightly so! The fall of the human race, innate sinfulness, and satanic influences have caused them to tread cautiously where possibility thinking seeks boldly to go. It is my prayer that the idea of reality thinking will address this dilemma and open the door for you to the power of God. Through Him you can find untapped power for healing, personal growth, and God-blessed success. Hopefully, together we will learn how to avoid the pitfalls of reaching too high, dreaming too long, or imagining too much. It is a way of thinking that we should allow to be sanctified by God's Spirit. Let God free us from human constraints yet always keep us in touch with the reality of His personal plan for our lives.

Throughout, I want us to remember this: It is more important that we determine God's purpose for our life than that we be successful by society's standards. It is more satisfying to know the riches of His love and the peace of His control, than to be prosperous or wealthy. If you don't believe this, ask someone who is celebrated or rich how happy they are. You may be very surprised by the answer. Unsanctified fame or wealth is merely a form of hell on earth. Who would deliberately set about creating it?

Why Reality Thinking?

What does one do when, with all the positive and possibility thoughts you have been able to muster, you don't accomplish your goal, achieve your success, or make your million? I suppose one could take refuge in any one or all of the following ideas.

- You could try to believe: "I would rather attempt to do something great and fail, than attempt to do nothing and succeed!" I find little comfort in this! The more I try and fail, the more likely I am to become disillusioned with life. I would rather attempt some great thing that I know I can realistically achieve.

• You could blame yourself for not thinking positively enough or allowing a sneaking thought of doubt to linger on the mind some sleepless night. But how can we be responsible for every fleeting idea or moment of disbelief? Some doubt is always bound to be around. The mind is only human, also. We can't expect it to function perfectly.

• You could blame God: "He let me down. He's not interested in me. He won't give me what I want because He's punishing me." Childish ideas, to say the least. Of course God is interested in you. He wouldn't be God if He weren't. But like a wise parent, He knows that what we want is not always what we need.

• You could take refuge in the idea that "delays are merely opportunities in disguise!" If this were true, I think I would go crazy! Can you imagine chasing every delay, frustration, obstacle, setback, and rejection as if it were some new opportunity? It would be like a dog chasing its tail.

No! The question of what to do when positive thinking fails doesn't have a simple answer. The problem is in the erroneous assumption that all you need for success is the right attitude and belief in yourself. Unfortunately, or perhaps fortunately, there is more to achievement than this. Sometimes it takes very hard work. Occasionally circumstances conspire against you and prevent you from reaching your dream. Not infrequently God has other plans for your life. Your success may thwart these plans. Can you blame Him if He has something better for you and therefore prevents you from being successful in some foolish personal scheme of your own? Our short-term, immediate goals don't always fit in with God's stable, long-term plans. It's just as well that many prayers for immediate success are never answered. God is wiser than to give us everything we ask for!

A Shattered Dream

I once knew a man in his early thirties who dreamed of owning his own business. He loved motorcycles, so combining this interest with his dream he borrowed money from parents, friends, and fellow church members and started a motorcycle sales and repair service.

He loved the adventure and excitement of selling. He believed he could be successful. He tithed his profits so that God would be on his side, taught Sunday School so that he could be of service to others, prayed and read his Bible so that he could be a spiritual person.

He was the model Christian businessman. He mastered all there was to know about how to be successful in business. He devoured the positive-thinking literature, took the Dale Carnegie courses, and most important of all he put them into practice.

And then a series of unfortunate and uncontrollable circumstances followed. The economy went sour. Within a matter of months his business was bankrupt.

As he thought about the prospect of telling his parents, friends, and fellow church members that their money was also gone, he came to only one conclusion: He had to end his life. He could not face living the rest of his life with this business failure on his conscience. The thought of looking into the faces of those who trusted him was too much to bear.

He shared his feelings with his lovely wife, who had just given birth to their first child. Somehow she persuaded him to consult me before he did anything drastic. When he came into my office his first words were, "Listen, doc, I'm only coming to see you this once to please my wife. I've had it with life and God! If this is how He treats those who try to serve Him, then He doesn't exist."

We talked about his feelings that first session—what it was like to feel abandoned and hopeless. We explored many questions: How could he be angry at God if God didn't exist? How would he kill himself if he followed through on his threat? Near the end of that first session I said to him, "God cannot be controlled by what we want out of life. We will only be happy and successful if we let Him give us what is best for us." He was intrigued by what I had said and agreed to see me again in a few days.

Slowly a therapeutic relationship developed. We explored his motives for wanting to be successful. He told me about his father, and how often the words "you're just a born loser, you'll never amount to anything" rang through his mind. He shared his fantasies of driving through his childhood neighborhood in a large limousine so that his success could be applauded by all his old friends. He began to realize that his prayers, tithing, and Christian service were his "bribes" to God to help him become successful. His positive thinking was a smoke screen designed to hide reality and deny his deep feelings of fearing to fail.

Finally he came to accept that his apparently catastrophic business failure was the greatest blessing God could have given him. Within a matter of months he wrapped up his business affairs and enrolled in a seminary. Today he and his wife serve as missionaries in a third-world country. He learned the greatest lesson any Christian could possibly learn: God's will and purpose for a life is always better than the noblest of dreams.

The Goals of Reality Thinking

There is one central goal in reality thinking. It is to maximize the potential for fulfilling God's plan for a given life. It is a way of thinking that constantly seeks to keep us in touch with God. It is thinking that seeks to remove every hindrance to finding out what God's plan is and how to achieve it. It is thinking that recognizes the inhibiting influences of early childhood training. It seeks to undo the negativity that so often breeds feelings of defeat and belief in helplessness. It seeks to free us from every encumbrance of defeatist thinking so that we may discern and fulfill God's perfect and complete plan for us.

The goals of reality thinking are *not* prosperity, wealth, and success, *unless* these are God's intentions for us. We can't all be wealthy. Only a few can be leaders. Some of us must be content to follow and do the best we can working with the hands God has given us.

The goal of reality thinking is *not* power. We are a power-hungry people. Our need (or greed) for wealth and success is often nothing more than a quest for control over others. This power is antithetical to Christian love. Are you surprised, therefore, if God doesn't always grant this power to people who can't use it properly?

The goal of reality thinking is *not* personal pride. You will never be able to sing with Frank Sinatra, "I did it my way," if God has a part in your success. At most you can whisper, "I made myself available so that He could do it through me." And you will be content with this.

No, reality thinking does not have prosperity as a goal, but authenticity and genuineness. Power is not the goal, but balance: a balance between the demands and reality of having to live in the here and now while eternity looms on the horizon. Personal pride is not the goal, but the preeminence of a Christ who denied Himself all personal ambition and power so that He could save a dying world. He must be lifted up and glorified at all times. He must eclipse our puny efforts. Above all, whatever success we may accomplish must be a demonstration of what His power can do through us, or else it is to no avail.

The Ingredients of Reality Thinking

Reality thinking attempts to bring together four very important systems:

1. The first, and most important, is **the Gospel's power to release us to be ourselves.** It is release from the destruction and power of sin and from the handicap and terror of our finitude. We have a finite number of years to our existence. We all know this. We also know that there is more to life than this life. Yet we all live as if nothing else mattered. To keep in touch with eternity

is to keep in touch with reality. Eternity keeps this mortal life in proper perspective.

2. The power of thoughts and the influence of our thinking. Thoughts are the most powerful controller of the human person. It is not without reason that Scripture places such strong emphasis on thoughts and beliefs. Thoughts have the power to make or break us. They shape our character and determine our destiny. They can heal us or infect us, bring us happiness or make us miserable. Sin, for example, is *first* a thought, *then* a deed. In reality thinking we are deeply concerned with how we think and use our thoughts.

3. The inhibiting influence of negative and defeatist thinking. Peale and Schuller are correct. Most of us are limited and restricted by negative thinking. We must find ways to undo these thinking patterns and to break free from years of helpless and hopeless habits of behavior. We must learn to transcend the artificial fences of negativity that keep us locked into dry and barren feeding grounds. These fences can be broken down. Many of them are only illusions.

4. The limitations of reality. Nothing is to be gained by ignoring reality. Deception is the end of all thinking that distorts or denies the realities of life. The danger in teaching people how to think of unlimited possibilities, to use success-generating imagination and obstacle-overcoming visual strategies is that it *may* create expectations that cannot be fulfilled. If they are tied to reality, then these strategies free you. If they are not, you will lose contact with reality and court disaster. This can easily distort the true nature of life. It can lead to a greater sense of failure or repeated frustrations and depression.

Reality thinking seeks to explore *all* possibilities, encourages positive rather than negative ideas, taps into the resources of God's limitless power, *but* encourages you to keep your feet on the ground and in touch with reality—the reality of God and the reality of life's limitations.

You *can* be everything God wants you to be. Let us together find out how.

Reality Thinking Puts God in Control

Chapter 3

Reality thinking is simply a way of ensuring that all we believe is tied as closely as possible to the world as it really is and to God as He has revealed Himself to us. In this chapter I would like to set out in more detail the principles of reality thinking.

For those who are accustomed to the term *positive thinking,* it may be that my emphasis on reality is bothersome. If you are someone who has tried for years to overcome a negative and constricted way of thinking and have finally found freedom in viewing life from a positive point of view, then this emphasis may create the feeling that you are being put back in your cage of negativity. Take heart! In no way does reality thinking stifle the achievement of your full freedom. It does not inhibit imagination or creativity. In fact, its effect should be quite the opposite! Reality thinking is not *less* than positive thinking, it is *more!* It is not a damper on enthusiasm but a higher-octane gas for more energy and personal mileage.

Reality Versus Unreality

It is Thomas Merton, in the opening remarks of his book *Thoughts in Solitude*, who says, "There is no greater disaster in the spiritual life than to be immersed in unreality." I say a loud *amen* to this, and I speak as a psychotherapist who for many years has tried to help Christian believers achieve healthy emotions. This is true not only for our spiritual life. I would say that there is no greater disaster in *any* aspect of life—physical, psychological, or spiritual—than to be immersed in unreality. When our life is determined by unreality, we must stagnate. When our life feeds off unreality, we must starve. There is nothing there to give or sustain *real* life. Unreality is a mirage in a dry and dusty desert. It gives the illusion that there is beauty and growth, but it soon vanishes when put to the test of life.

Our world tends to create much unreality and presents it to us as if it were reality. Movies, novels, TV, and even some preachers, present us with a distorted and unrealistic picture of love, life, prosperity, and success. We either live our lives as one long fantasy or with a deep, though often unconscious, resentment that life is not being fair to us. We are not getting out of life what our heroes are getting. Someone else always has it better, if not in real life then on the screen. Contentment is a rare quality in twentieth-century civilized Christendom. The experience of the Apostle Paul who knew that contentment had to be learned in "whatsoever" circumstances life had to offer is seldom seen nowadays because it is hard to be satisfied when surrounded by the unreality of an artificial world.

One of the greatest gifts you can give yourself is the gift of reality. To renounce an illusory world and experience living in direct contact with the "givens" of life is vital to mental and spiritual health. The changing circumstances of life, the growing old and finally of dying, all give life a new meaning when we live fully accepting their reality. Every minute becomes precious. Little time is spent wishing that things were different and no time is wasted if it can be avoided. Appreciate life for what it really is, and you will find a new thrill in living. I can recall a rather extreme example of this. A patient I saw many years ago (let's call him Frank) was on the verge of suicide. His life was a total wreck. At thirty-six years of age he had experienced nothing but pain and misery for most of his life.

When he was sixteen, he was erroneously diagnosed as paranoid schizophrenic because of a series of angry encounters with school teachers he felt did not understand him. For many years following, he was treated, quite unsuccessfully, by a series of psychiatrists. He wanted to make a success of life. He was very intelligent, had completed two master's degrees, but would not come to terms with his periodic outbursts of rage. He wished he were someone else. In fact, he would spend many hours lying on his bed and fantasizing that he was a great business tycoon.

I suspected that his real problem was some minor brain damage. This could, I believe, account for his rage attacks and sometimes bizarre behavior. A neurological examination proved I was right. But how would Frank take the news? On the one hand there was treatment available to control his behavior. On the other, he would always have this damage.

When I told Frank, he was ecstatic. At last he understood what was wrong. He could live with reality—he couldn't, with the confusion and uncertainty of not knowing what was wrong. The treatment proved successful, and even though he will have to take medication the rest of his life, he is now a contented and happy human being.

Reality is the solid foundation for all of life. We must come to terms with and be accepting of what is truly real.

What Is Unreality?

When I speak of "unreality," I am, of course, using a relative term. Some aspects of life are unreal relative to others. They are less important, if they exist at all. Ultimately, we must accept that all material things (money, homes, cars, jobs, and health) are relatively unreal alongside eternal and spiritual things. A

Ambivalence toward success: Saint Paul — "can possibly get it, but don't be too frustrated if you don't"

healthy spirituality constantly keeps this perspective in mind. If not, despair is likely to be the dominant mood.

Furthermore, even among material things, some are unreal in relation to others. It is far more important that my wife be in good health than that I keep $10,000 hoarded away in a savings account that could be spent on her medical care. When confronted by certain choices between relative material things, I don't hesitate to make my decision in favor of greater reality.

And this is the essence of reality thinking: I know what is more important and I make choices based on this knowledge. Let us explore further what it means to think like this.

Reality Thinking Is Positive

You will gather from what I have said thus far that reality thinking is always positive. But it is not always positive in the sense that it overlooks or denies the *real* negatives of life.

Unfortunately, many who have adopted a positive-thinking attitude have merely shifted to another form of thinking, often neurotic, by adopting what psychologists call denial. *Denial* is a defense mechanism designed to keep our anxiety at a minimum. It avoids reality by refusing to look it in the face. In other words, when confronted by a troublesome and anxiety-producing situation, instead of looking realistically at all aspects (both positive and negative), people who use denial look just at the positive and ignore the negative. For them it doesn't exist. They block out any awareness of the negative and they may even exaggerate the positive so much as to make it more attractive. The positive, then, also becomes unreality.

I recently helped a couple through a difficult life decision. Paul, the husband, was in his mid-forties and had become thoroughly bored with his life as an engineer. He wanted to make a change to a more exciting and demanding work situation. One day he heard that a business was for sale and tried to convince his wife that they should sell their home, take their savings, buy the business, and move to New York. She refused. She

look at Schuller: Positive

Contingent connections — between spirituality & success, creates uncertainty — "God may bless" — so have to be open to "possibilities" was convinced that it was a bad decision. There was too much risk involved. Both had prayed much about the matter. She said God had told her not to go, while he claimed God was telling him they should go. Who was right? Both claimed God's direct leading. He accused her of being too negative and she accused him of being foolhardy! So they came to see me. The conflict was destroying their marriage.

As we explored the issue together, it became clear that Paul, in his eagerness to make a change, was looking at the whole deal too positively. He was given to denial and, typically, he was refusing to weigh the negatives. There were obvious blind spots in the way he looked at the venture, and he dismissed as petty, all his wife's arguments against going. I thought she had good business sense. She knew a little about cash-flow problems, carrying too much debt, and so on. He was far too impulsive and impatient and had not taken the time to check out other prospects.

We compromised and I finally convinced Paul that he needed to look realistically at some other possibilities as well. One week later they returned to see me, both smiling broadly. Within days of our counseling session they had heard of another business offer. The terms were infinitely better, the risks less, they didn't have to move their home, and both were united in believing that they were making the right decision to purchase this business.

This is not to say that reality thinking never takes risks. Of course it does. But it does not gamble on achieving success when the odds against success are hopeless. No amount of positive thinking will overcome obvious obstructions over which you have no control. If you fail to look at all the obstacles before you take your plunge, don't be surprised if you fail.

If you have openly examined every obstacle and realistically appraised their strengths and then decided to risk your venture, you have a greater possibility of being successful. To deny or ignore obstacles in the name of positive thinking is stupidity, not wisdom.

Also, God is the God of order and disorder. When two people

earnestly seek His guidance on a life-changing decision, I would expect to find unity in the conviction about His will. When there is no unity then I suspect it is because unreal thinking is getting in the way for one of the parties.

Reality Thinking Is Not Impulsive

I recall watching a series on "Masterpiece Theatre" that told the story of soldiers disarming bombs during the Second World War blitz on London. Imagine a soldier having to disarm a bomb, looking at it all over and discovering that the fuse mechanism was different from any other he had seen. As he looks at it, he asks himself, "Should I proceed to remove the fuse? What if it doesn't behave like the others I've taken out?"

These soldiers had orders not to disarm bombs that were different from those previously defused. Clear procedures had been worked out for every bomb the Nazis had devised thus far. Any new bomb discovered needed to be carefully researched. No one was to take unnecessary risks. Yet many of these soldiers looked at the strange fuses and believed they could do the job of defusing anyway. The consequences were disastrous.

The human mind easily succumbs to impulse responses. We readily jump at escaping from reality and wishing things were different. I can well understand why many of the soldiers said to themselves, "Let's try it. I'm sure it will be OK." Taking unnecessary risks through impulsive behavior is *not* reality thinking. It is absurd thinking. Yet it is common for all of us to think this way about many things.

Reality Thinking Is Creative

Life is an obstacle course, it seems, and living is like running an obstacle course. I know no one who is successful who has not had to overcome significant obstacles in the path of their progress toward success by being creative in their thinking.

It stands to reason, doesn't it, that success is a matter of knowing how to overcome obstacles? If it weren't, then everyone would be successful.

What prevents success, therefore, is mostly an inability to overcome the frustrations and hindrances that are inevitable in every program, project, or goal. Only those who can overcome them get to succeed.

Obstacles are of many sorts. There are internal obstacles, such as your shy personality, quick temper, or lack of courage, and there are external obstacles, such as the bad economy, uncooperative people, or bad timing. There are *always* obstacles—this is the given. I see reality thinking as a way of being creative whenever we are confronted by obstacles. Reality thinking deals with obstacles by responding to them as challenges to be overcome, not as handicaps to which one must surrender or as reasons for depression.

Reality thinking is therefore an *attitude*. It looks at the resistance of others, the barriers of negativity, and the hindrances of uncontrolled circumstances and says, "This thing that is stopping me *can* be overcome." It then asks, "What must I do to remove or work around it?" After a while, obstacles are welcomed. They represent a test of your creative abilities, so you don't resent them. You receive them gladly. They are the challenges that add zest to life. They send your mind forth in all directions to search for creative ideas and solutions. They expand your experience, causing you to keep an open mind, always observing, analyzing, considering, and questioning, until you find the hidden key that unlocks the problem.

Take a moment right now to reflect on the hindrances in your own life. Examine the obstacles that prevent you from achieving your goals. Categorize them by writing them down on paper under the following headings:

INTERNAL
- Personality traits
- Faulty beliefs
- Expectations

- Education
- Habits
- Physique
- Other

EXTERNAL
- People
- Money
- Relatives
- Spouse
- Boss or supervisor
- Subordinates
- Children
- Parents
- Other circumstances

Now examine your list. Take each obstacle in turn and list two or three ways in which you can remove, overcome, or work around the obstacle. For example, let us suppose you are having difficulty getting the right sort of job. You've spent hours writing letters, sending resumés and making phone calls—all to no avail. Examine the list of hindrances above, and list those you think might be a problem. As you look at internal factors, perhaps you realize that you do not have the right qualifications for the job you want and that your attitude is not right. You come across angry and demanding, expecting others to appreciate you for what you are and not for what you can do.

Look at external factors. Perhaps the letters of recommendation you are using are not adequate. Your previous supervisor did a poor job and never stressed your strong points.

What can you do? Plan a program for improving your education. Enroll in an evening class and show evidence of this in your job application. Change your attitude. Others don't have to employ you—they don't owe you anything. Be a more likeable person. Go to your previous supervisor and ask him or her to give you another letter. List the points you would like stressed. Strategize. Plan a campaign. Imagine that you are a general fighting a battle. Set out the steps you must take to overcome the hindrance.

Get into the habit of shifting into a strategy-planning mode every time you encounter an obstacle. Practice with minor as well as major issues; do it every day, and soon it will become a habit. Obstacles will bring out the best of you in creativity thinking, if you let them.

Reality Thinking Takes Control

Life has a way of turning us into victims. A *victim* is one who is cheated or suffers at the hands of others. You can be a victim not only of a crime, but of neglect or the control others exert over you. Victims suffer whenever they find themselves under the control of others. They never feel that they control their own destiny. Others, or circumstances, are in control.

Christians should always, under Christ, be in control of themselves. Since we are responsible for our own life and must give an account of it, we cannot allow others to determine our beliefs, actions, or feelings. We must be free of the manipulations and controls of everyone except God.

I realize that this is not easy! We are so caught up and conditioned by a need to please others that we easily surrender control over what we want to be and do—to them. The wages are small but, somehow, pleasing others seems to pay more handsomely than pleasing ourselves.

Also, we are called to "serve" and love others and to be self-sacrificing—and this is right. But many of us are not sacrificing ourselves but are allowing ourselves to be used and manipulated in such a way that we don't honor Christ but rather discredit Him.

We are controlled by "what will so-and-so think?" We are inhibited by fears of offending others and will often rather suffer emotional pain ourselves than confront someone who is hurting us. This is not an act of sacrifice but an act of cowardice. We do things we really don't want to do simply because we don't have the courage to say a simple no. Ministers are, unfortunately, the most frequently abused people in this regard. They don't always feel they have the liberty to stand up for themselves and the word no is difficult to utter. If they were responsible only for themselves, this would not be such an issue. But spouses and children often have to suffer from neglect because of the minister's fear of what others might think if he or she stops being a victim.

There is a healthy way to sacrifice yourself—and an unhealthy way. Remember that sacrifice is only meaningful and healthy when what you are giving is yours to give. It must be free! It must be unencumbered. It must be willingly given—or else the giving of it only breeds resentment.

When you give yourself in a loving way to another, whether it be your time, money, or talent, you must also have the freedom not to give it—otherwise it is not a sacrifice; it is extortion. You have no choice! You are too afraid not to give because you don't know how your refusal will be received. You are afraid that you will not be liked or loved in return if you do not give of yourself every time it is demanded. This can lead to deep-seated feelings of anger and is unhealthy, both to your spiritual and psychological well-being.

Reality thinking is a way of removing yourself from the traps of being victimized. It demands that you stop being controlled by what others will think and that you take control of your own destiny, your actions and reactions, so that you can be free to do what you believe God wants you to do. Don't do this in blatant disregard for the feelings of others. Do it in a spirit of gentleness and kindness. You will then find a new joy in the actions of self-sacrifice that you know you are being called upon to make. You may need to change your attitude about how others control you, so ask yourself the following questions whenever you are being confronted by a situation that demands your time or energy.

- Do I give others too much control over my time, energy, and activities? Do I feel any resentment about this?

- Do I fear rejection by others if I do not do what they want me to do?
- Do I often take the blame for things that happen to others?
- When someone else is gloomy and miserable, do I tend to become that way also?
- Do I often agree to do things I really don't want to do?
- Am I subject to a lot of petty rules about my life which have no meaning but am too afraid to change for fear that someone else will be offended?
- Do I respond too easily to sales talk or the plausible arguments others give me as to why I should do what they want me to do?
- Do I receive criticism by becoming totally devastated and then surrender myself to do what is wanted of me?
- Am I always apologizing, whether I am guilty of any wrongdoing or not?

If you can honestly say no to all of these questions, you are also an unusually assertive person.

Don't be too surprised if you answer many of these questions with a yes. To some extent we are all guilty of being victimized in this way. The fewer yes's you can give to these questions the better, so make it your goal to work at any of the responses you agree are not healthy.

To remedy the tendency to become a victim, begin by changing your belief about what it means to sacrifice yourself. Dispose of the idea that others must always come first regardless of the circumstances. Think rather that you have a *choice* in every demand situation and that provided you are not robbing another of his or her rights you have a right to choose your own direction as you believe God has led you. If you choose to sacrifice your rights in a given situation, make sure that you are aware of having made that choice. You can't have your cake and eat it! You can't sacrifice yourself freely and then complain about how demanding and inconsiderate others are. If you feel they are demanding, then choose *not* to sacrifice yourself.

By carefully working at changing your attitude you can change the way you handle other people. There are times when I don't want to do what my wife wants me to do. It may be going somewhere or performing some chore. While I can choose not to comply with her request (and I have done this on rare occasions), if I allow myself to follow through on her request without changing my thoughts about it, I feel resentful. This resentment is unnecessary and harmful to our relationship. So I stop my thoughts and say to myself, "My wife wants me to do something for her. I can choose not to do it or I can comply. Even though I don't want to do it, I freely choose to do it because I love her." After a few such "self-talks" my general attitude begins to change. I begin to think this way automatically and I hardly have to pay attention to my self-talk. Now, when I comply with a request from my wife, there is no resentment at all. I am free to choose either way. Such a change in attitude can have a dramatic effect on the residual feelings of anger that so often lie hidden from view in many marriages.

Reality Thinking Is Honest

Throughout this book the word *reality* should be taken as synonymous with *honest.* In this sense it means to be "sincere, truthful, and genuine."

The Apostle Paul ends his second epistle to the Corinthians by defending his apostleship and calling his readers to self-examination. He says these words, "Now I pray to God that ye do no evil; not that we should appear approved, but that ye should do that which is honest . . ." (13:7).

In the context of the previous verses Paul was saying that he did not want to be vindicated. He was not concerned about his reputation even to the extent that he should seem discredited. Disregarding his pride he wanted his readers to be *honest.* He wanted them to do what was right in their eyes.

Genuineness should be a quality that characterizes every Christian. No success is worth achieving if it robs you of this priceless gift or if you must surrender it as the cost. Reality thinking insists that you be honest about yourself, thoroughly genuine and perfectly frank. Any distortion of these realities will only bring disillusionment and disappointment.

Thinking honestly about oneself is not easy. In our culture we tend to distort our self-image. We feel that everyone else is expendable. We are the only ones who are not. Our desire for success is often merely a desire for self-glorification. If we were to redesign the world, we would probably fill it with clones of ourselves.

To look honestly at oneself takes tremendous courage. It requires that we strip away all the facade and make-believe we've developed over the years to give us a false feeling of self-esteem, and then accept what is left, even if it is not pretty!

To look honestly at oneself requires that we have some ability to "step outside." God has given us, as humans, this capacity for self-reflection. The children of God have always been called to review who they are and what they want to be. In Jeremiah's Lamentations over the misery of Jerusalem he invites the people thus: "Let us search and try our ways, and turn again to the Lord" (Lamentations 3:40). Paul also tells us, "Examine yourselves, whether ye be in the faith: prove your own selves . . ." (2 Corinthians 13:5).

But not only must we be honest about ourselves, we must also be honest about our world. It is a great but erroneous myth that somehow through "mind over matter" we can create and control the world so that it can become anything we want it to be. While it is true that much of our world is of our own making, there are very obvious limits to what we can do. The truly successful person is able, often with remarkable clarity, to realistically evaluate the limitations of the world around him or her *and then* take the necessary steps to overcome these limitations. Such a person does not sit in an armchair and say, "Well, if I believe strongly enough all my obstacles will go away." They won't! The successful person plans and strategizes ways to overcome the obstacles and always takes reality into account.

The unsuccessful person does not like obstacles. They get in the way! They are limitations that provoke anger. They take energy! They demand time. They take effort to overcome! So he or she settles down to live a trivial life, devoid of imagination and creativity. It is very easy to be unsuccessful. Success, on the other hand, makes demands that only a few are willing to tackle.

Reality Thinking Is Christ Minded

While there is much more that can be said about the nature of reality thinking, and I will continue in later chapters to elaborate on these ideas, let me conclude this chapter with some thoughts on the mind of Christ.

As a psychologist I cannot but be greatly impressed by the accounts of Christ's thinking. His mind, while on earth, was extraordinary by human standards. So much so that we are clearly directed to "Let this mind be in you, which was also in Christ Jesus" (Philippians 2:5). It is our duty, therefore, to know the mind of Christ and to emulate it with His help. Verse two of this great "mind of Christ chapter" (Philippians 2) also invites us to "be likeminded."

Reflect with me for a moment on the nature of Christ's mind. In the description given in verses 2 to 9, we are told that Christ's mind was a:

- Loving mind ("having the same love"), verse 2.
- Godly mind ("equal with God"), verse 6.
- Servant mind ("the form of a servant"), verse 7.
- Humble mind ("he humbled himself"), verse 8.
- Obedient mind ("and became obedient unto death"), verse 8.
- Exalted mind ("God also hath highly exalted him"), verse 9.

If you examine the accounts of Jesus' actions and conversations as given in the Gospels, you will discover that He exemplified every one of these qualities. He was the perfect example of everything He calls us to be!

But what of us? Do you not desire these qualities? I certainly do. Can we live up to these standards? Dare we not live up to them? I believe that if we set our mind to it, we can develop a Christ-like mind. This is His gift to us. We need to be willing to receive it.

Reality Thinking Puts God in Control

When I was in my middle teens, a Christian friend gave me a book to read that shook my young mind to the core and left me forever affected by it. It was Charles Sheldon's novel, *In His Steps*. It moved me deeply and was one of the instruments that brought me to Christ. As a young sixteen-year-old my life was confused, I was unhappy and ready for direction, and the message of the book struck home at a deep level.

What has stayed with me down through the years are these words: "What would Jesus do?" The stories of the various people depicted in the novel all revolve around answers to this question and how these answers impact their lives. For months my head reeled with those words. Today they frequently come to my mind. "What would Jesus do?" What would He do if this was His child causing all the trouble at school? What would He do if this was His neighbor's dog creating so much disturbance? What would He do if His boss was so crabby and always picking on Him? What would He do if His sermon was criticized by a senior elder or if someone didn't like the way He dressed? To take this question seriously can have a revolutionary effect on your life. Try it and see for yourself!

If we use reality thinking, we should constantly be asking this question: "What would Jesus do?"

Don't you often long to know what Christ thinks? How He thinks? What a difference it would make to our lives if we earnestly tried to discover His mind for many of our life situations.

"What would Jesus do in this situation?" By asking this question we can avoid many mistakes and prevent much pain because it prompts us to stop and discover Christ's mind.

It has been my experience that when I do stop and ask myself this question, Christ is there to give me an answer. He has not left us without a Comforter who "shall teach you all things, and bring all things to your remembrance, whatsoever I have said unto you" (John 14:26).

In the final analysis, reality thinking puts God more in control of your life. You become more aware of your limitations and the limitations of human existence, so that you place more trust in God and seek His purpose for your life; and this is as it should be.

Is the Sky Your Real Limit?

Chapter 4

Very few people ever attain their full potential. I suppose many of us know this from personal experience! We are told that the best of us barely tap a fraction of the power of the human brain. No matter how "self-actualized" someone may appear on the outside, there is always room for more growth and personal development on the inside.

While this is true for people in general, it is particularly true for the Christian, who can tap into resources quite outside the realm of the physical. When a person who is a Christian opens fully to the power of God, the potential for human good and the glory of the Kingdom of God is mind boggling. But few of us really open ourselves to this power. Through ignorance or fear we live constricted and inhibited lives. These constrictions and inhibitions are generally not caused by physical limitations. They are the product of our faulty thinking and inadequate beliefs.

Legitimates Jesus.

Jesus used as a metaphor

Spiritual Investments

If there is one important lesson that the parable of the talents (Matthew 25:14–30) teaches us, it is that God has endowed us with certain gifts or responsibilities with which He expects us to "turn a profit." A *talent,* in New Testament language, is a fairly large sum of money. By today's standards it would probably be valued at about $1,000. It was serious investment, not a game they were playing. Jesus was deliberate in His intention on this point. The money was given to each servant "according to his several ability" (verse 15). *All* were expected to be profitable.

expected to try hard, do all we can

It is important for us to understand that God is in the investment business. Our existence on this earth is not just a game. We are not idly whiling away the time until it is all over. It is serious business—this matter of living. He is interested in making spiritual investments and gives to each of us "gifts differing according to the grace that is given to us ..." (Romans 12:6). He expects us to turn a profit.

I prefer to think of the talents He distributes to us as "grace gifts" for very important reasons. First, when all is over and done with and we are called to give an account of ourselves and how we have used our gifts, we will not be able to claim any of the glory for ourselves. Our accomplishments will be God glorifying. When we display our profits and the gains are counted, it will be clear to all that it was His grace and power that accomplished the increase.

Second, they are grace gifts because no gift is unimportant. There may, by the world's standards, be lesser gifts and greater gifts. Some will be very important while others not so important. Many will be very public while others will be very private. But in God's sight they will *all* be crucial to the functioning of the body of Christ and the extension of His Kingdom.

Third, they are grace gifts because hungry and desperately needy people are drawn to them and find power to be healed and liberated. Such a gift not only blesses you but benefits all those who come into contact with you.

Last, they are grace gifts because there is only one dynamic force behind them. This is not the force of some "Jedi" or other space object or civilization. It is the power of the one and only true God who works in us through the Holy Spirit to "quicken our mortal bodies" and "help our infirmities" (*see* Romans 8:11, 26). Let us receive our talents as gifts of grace. If we do, then we also receive God's power to fulfill these gifts.

Where Are the Talents?

After many years in the Christian psychotherapist's chair, listening to the problems of many devout pastors and Christians, I must sadly confess that the majority of us turn out to be "unprofitable servants." Sad, isn't it? But such is human nature. Instead of the joy of creative service, many get bogged down by meaningless drudgery. Instead of freedom in ministry, most create working prisons for themselves. Instead of feeling courageous and adventuresome, there is a strong desire to hide our talents because we are afraid (Matthew 25:25). We haven't changed much since New Testament times. Two thousand years from now, we will probably still do the same!

The unprofitable servant in this parable does an interesting thing when he presents his excuse for failing. In psychological parlance, he "projects" himself into his image of his master. He says: "Lord, I knew thee that thou art an hard man, reaping where thou has not sown, and gathering where thou has not strawed: and I was afraid, and went and hid thy talent in the earth . . ." (Matthew 25:24,25).

This is *not* what his lord was like. It wasn't his master he was afraid of, it was *himself.* He was afraid of failing, so he wouldn't risk anything. He didn't believe he could succeed, so he didn't try. And even if he did mistakenly believe that his master was a hard taskmaster, the parable goes on to show that he was obligated to try even harder and thus earn his master's praise. But he didn't.

If you are wondering why you feel you are a failure, you may not need to look beyond this parable for an answer. Jesus is describing a universal problem. The solution, as we shall see in the next section, lies with us.

Denying Our Gifts

The unprofitable servant was afraid of himself! I must sympathize with him because so often I feel as if this is my own experience. I suspect that most of my readers feel the same way.

The root problem is not that God hasn't given us gifts we can use or responsibilities we must fulfill, but that we are too afraid to assume them. We create obstacles that don't allow His gifts to be expressed through us. This is the problem in a nutshell!

We deny the expression of His gifts through our fears, distorted self-image, lack of courage, and self-destructive style of thinking. And God will *not* willy-nilly override these obstacles. What would be the point if He did? We are not called to be puppets-on-a-string or robots-controlled-by-a-supercomputer. God does not take away our free will when we become Christians. This would be tantamount to taking away reality. No, we are called as free-willed agents. Free to accept or reject His gifts. But we must also give an account of our dealings in due course. So in this respect we are responsible for who we are, even though He indwells us.

This is reality! We will never be able to say to God, "Well, I did it because You made me do it." Our behavior is always a choice, made by free-willed minds. The wonderful thing is that if I stay close to God, I make choices that are responsible and in His will—but they are always my choices and I will be held responsible for them.

Fear of Failure

The greatest single fear we have to overcome if we are going to be holistically successful is our fear of failing. The fear of failure is very real and is deeply ingrained in all of us through our cul-

ture. We live in a part of the world that values success and suc-
ceeding above everything else. So much so that it creates in many
a hopeless "I'm never going to make it" syndrome. Unfortunately, he who hopes to avoid all failure is living in a world of
unreality.

To be free to exercise your gifts and be fully what God intends
you to be, you must face one solid reality of this world: Some
failure is inevitable. And you cannot let your fear of failure stifle
your creativity and freedom if you are going to be successful.

Many years ago a friend taught me a truth I have never forgotten. I had failed at some task and was sitting in my office
brooding over my disappointment when he came by on a brief
visit. He listened to my tale of woe and then said just four words
and left. The words were: *Failure is for growing.* What he meant
was that failure points out errors in your behavior or judgment
so you can correct them. The truth drove home like a bullet, and
I have always remembered these words. Failure gives you the
feedback you need so that corrective adjustments can be made.
Most scientists know this. They will concede that the best research they can perform is 90 percent failure, 9 percent luck, and
1 percent planned success. The 90 percent failure is very important. It helps them to plan for the next success. It leads the way to
the next step. Without it there would be no progress.

I love target shooting. Recently I bought a telescope for my
rifle so that I could learn to shoot at distant targets. When I first
fitted the telescope to the rifle and tried shooting at a nearby target, I failed hopelessly. I could not find a single bullet hole in the
paper target after thirty or forty shots!

I was despondent. I could have felt like a failure, condemned
myself for being useless, and thrown the gun and scope in the
trash can. But I knew better! Slowly, by observing where my
misses were going, I adjusted the vertical and horizontal align-
ments of the telescope's cross hairs. One hundred shots later I
was centering on the target and hitting the bull's-eye every time.
My failures taught me how to correct my rifle's behavior.

In both the physical and spiritual spheres of my life, failures serve a very important purpose. Successful people know how to use their failures to correct their beliefs, behavior, and attitudes. They know they can only become "centered" if they are willing to learn from their errors. But if we are not willing to risk failing, or if we are totally devastated by failure, we can easily bury our solitary talent and become a "wicked and slothful servant." I cannot expect God to be pleased with this.

Realizing You Have Gifts

I believe with the great British preacher of the last century, Charles Spurgeon, that our gifts and talents are a reflection of who we were created to be. God's calling corresponds to the reality of who we truly are. God does not call us to be great scientists if we do not have scientific intelligence or to be great preachers if we lack the oratory skills for this. While He has gifts for all of us, He does not give us all the same gift.

This is not to say that we cannot be surprised by what God can do through us. A stammering, stuttering Moses can become a great leader in God's hands, but this is only because God knew the true potential that lay deep within the person of Moses. Many, if not most, of us have untapped, unrecognized, and unfulfilled gifts waiting to be brought to light. Just as great sculptors can bring out the buried form or figure within a block of marble, God waits and longs to bring out the best in each of us.

Each work of His grace has a limitation imposed upon it by our readiness and willingness to participate. God does not make us what we are not. He cuts away that which disfigures and inhibits us until our real beauty is brought to life for all to see. Others then marvel and glorify God as they say, "Do you mean to tell me that that is the same person I went to school with? I can't believe it!"

I must stress this point because too many Christians get caught up in false and unrealistic dreams about who they want to be. They try to impose on God their specification for the gift they want. This is where the meaning of the phrase "to every man according to his several ability" in the parable of the talents is so important (Matthew 25:15). Romans 12:6 and 1 Corinthians 12:4 also remind us that our gifts differ according to God's grace. *God does not make us what we are not.* The sky is not our limit. In one sense we have a limit that is higher than the sky. But in another sense we cannot expect to become just anything we want or desire. God brings to light what we are to become by the liberating power of His Holy Spirit—if we will let Him.

I was only a teenager when Billy Graham began his great evangelistic career. When I, growing up in far-off Africa, heard broadcasts of the early Billy Graham Crusades, I would get lost in the fantasy of being a great preacher. At the age of eighteen I was already preaching regularly and conducting youth evangelism services. On one occasion, at a camp for young people, I gave an invitation for those who wanted to accept Christ to come forward and seventeen of sixty or seventy young people responded. I believed I had found my hidden "talent," and pursued this for a while. Very soon I was to discover that I was wrong! It was only my hungry ego needing stroking that called me. I wanted the glory but not the hard work, the applause without the criticisms. And God slowly guided me away from preaching to my present ministry. I had to learn the lesson that God's gifts are not arbitrary and limitless nor do they feed our neurotic needs. God does not heal our pathological hunger for love and attention by giving us power and adoring followers. His gifts heal the source of the problem; they don't just alleviate the symptoms. He prefers radical surgery to ameliorating ointment.

At the same time we can be running away from God's calling, just as Moses did, when we refuse to face the reality of who we can become. It may be that God *is* calling you to some great task. The talents within you lie waiting to be discovered and released. Don't waste too much time looking elsewhere and wanting to be someone else. You may fail to discover the gift that God has blessed you with, because it is staring you in the face.

Understanding Your Talents

To help you understand what happens when you try to discover your unique potential, examine the following diagram.

I have shown the various levels of your potential as a series of concentric circles. At the center, the bull's-eye, is the real you—where you are now. It is a given that you are not fully developed and have not yet accomplished the goals and dreams of your calling. In psychological language, you are still "underactualized" and striving to become what you are capable of becoming. If you are a Christian, this "becoming" is tied directly to God's plan and purpose for your life.

Everyone constantly changes, for better or for worse. This inner circle representing where you are now is, therefore, constantly changing. It shrinks when you retreat from God's pur-

THE BOUNDARIES OF REALITY

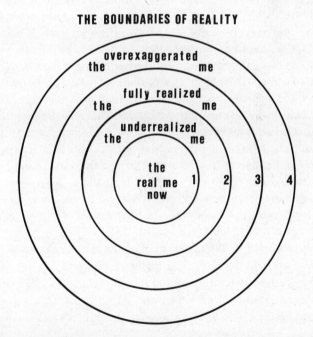

pose and expands when you collaborate and become God's person. When you are growing, your actions are positive and produce more growth. When you are shrinking, your actions are negative and self-destructive.

The Underactualized Person

The second circle, which is outside of where you are now, reflects the typical boundary of the average person, Christian or otherwise. This represents the limits of a constricted, negative-thinking, inhibited, and fearful person. This circle could even be smaller than the first circle. It is the "underrealized" or "underactualized" you. This you is caused by fear and the super self-protectiveness that prevents risk taking and that is morbidly preoccupied with not failing. It also thrives on a poor understanding of your real limitations. You feel so little respect for yourself that you can hardly trust God to love you.

I encountered an example of such thinking recently in a young man (let's call him Peter) who was brought up in a wealthy home, surrounded by every luxury you can imagine. It was not just the affluent environment that created his problems. Many children of wealthy and successful parents have the advantage of being exposed to the right style of thinking, so they have realistic ideas and a better understanding of their potential than other children. Peter had failed to realize what his realistic limitations were. He had flunked out in high school and spent his days lying around the house or ogling girls at the local beach.

When finally confronted with pressure from his father to do something with his life, Peter tried his hand at a few jobs but failed at everything except janitorial work. It was sad to listen to his feelings of frustration when he finally realized that success in life required hard work!

"Why can't I be the president of a company like my dad?" he would ask. He could not accept the limitations of life, of his lower-than-average intellect and his limited abilities. When encouraged to go back to school and improve his basic skills, he would become very angry, almost to the point of having a rage attack, and accuse his parents of deliberately not wanting him to be a success. His understanding of how he could achieve his true potential was grossly distorted. A long period of psychotherapy was needed to restore reality to his thinking.

This underrealized potential characterizes the majority of people. Inferiority feelings are epidemic and defeatist thinking predominates. And it is to this group that the ideas of positive and possibility thinking appeal the most. This way of thinking frees them from the bondage of their early upbringing and cultural prisons. It teaches them not to trust their feelings of helplessness and uselessness. It helps them to escape from the feelings of destructiveness and puts them in charge of their life circumstances once more.

Your True Potential

The third circle represents the boundary of our true, maximum, realistic potential. There *is* a limit to what we can become, so let us accept this. For some it will be more than others, just as one servant receives five talents and another, two.

There is always the danger of believing that there is no boundary at all to what you can become. This creates a distorted and exaggerated idea of what you can do with your life and may lead to much frustration and disappointment. The fourth circle represents the boundary of a person's unrealistic and exaggerated potential. While it is shown beyond the "fully realized" circle, it really does not exist at all. It is the product of imagination, unfulfilled neurotic needs, and unrealistic self-expectations. It is only a fantasy. It is way beyond realistic accomplishment and only serves to increase the pain of real failure. People with too much circle 4 are often unhappy and depression prone.

The Two Errors of Self-Growth

My model for understanding the boundaries of personal development and the discovery of talents shows how two errors of self-growth can occur.

1. The first is to become an underrealized self. Your goal is limited to circle 2, a little beyond where you are now. You don't believe in yourself. You lack self-confidence. People walk all over you. You don't believe that you can accomplish anything significant in this life. Everything seems to go wrong and you are afraid to risk new goals or behaviors, meet new people, or respond to new challenges. If you live at this level, you are bound to be unhappy, depressed, and feel unfulfilled most of the time.

Since you don't expect much from yourself, one would wonder why you would not be happy and contented. Your goals are so easy to achieve that you hardly have to get out of your armchair! The truth is that even though you make few demands of yourself, underrealized people are seldom truly happy or spiritually contented. It's like being a balloon that is only half-inflated. You look all crinkly and ugly. You are not being stretched to your beautiful limit. You remain limp and useless. Such is the underachiever. He or she is the "unprofitable servant" hiding his talent in some secret place. If this is you, then you need to set yourself free, dig up your talent, and get back into the business of life.

2. The second error of self-growth is to escape from the reality of what your true self can become and develop an overexaggerated self. This sort of person is heading for disappointment and disaster. He or she has leapt over the boundary of their true talents. They usually live a life of fantasy and escape in circle 4. They always dream of victory—but never experience it. They think of some great accomplishment and don't lift a finger to move toward it.

They are also miserable! Like the underachiever, the overachiever is never contented. How can such people be happy if they are constantly confronted with unfulfilled and exaggerated goals?

Herein lies the danger of much success-oriented positive thinking. It may give the illusion of freeing you from a constricted and negative self but take you beyond reality to dreams

of unrealistic impossibilities. You walk out of a prison of negativity only to find yourself in the abyss of a black hole.

Somewhere between, with feet, heart, and mind deeply
grounded in God's caring love and liberating grace, you will find
the true reality of all you can be. It is a glorious and beautiful reality, with every intrinsic promise opened to you without frustration or fear of failure.

In our ultimate accountability to God we will be judged by reality and not by our alleged perception of reality. We will not be
able to say, "But I did not know." God will hold us accountable
for not finding out what His will is.

God's limits are our limits. We are happiest when we live in
full harmony with them. His limits are not onerous. They are
tailored to our unique characteristics. God intends us to follow
His limits and find in them a freedom to be our true selves. This
is what holistic success is all about. It is achieved through realistic thinking and is open to *every* Christian.

Claiming Your Full Potential

The territory between the "real you" and the boundary of the
fully realizable you must be discovered and occupied. This is
unclaimed territory. It is yours for the asking. God offers it to
you and invites you to pursue its discovery. He will give you the
wisdom to discern what it is if you trust Him. Nurture and develop it. Water and enrich it with God's Spirit. It belongs to no
one but you. No one else can claim this promised land—but you.
Your purpose in God's eternal plan is unique. It is unprece-
dented and to be found in no one else. Your potentiality in God
is never recurring. No one in the future will have it; not your
children nor their children. This is the glory of God's perfect
plan. Make sure you don't pass it up.

Having just reread the parable of the talents again, I am struck
with the fact that the saddest part of the story is that the unprofitable servant has his one and only talent *taken away* and given to
the servant who is faithful. Does this mean that grace gifts that

are not employed are lost to those for whom they were originally intended? I think it does! It's not that others gain but that you lose! Grace may be free and undeserved, but it will not allow itself to be wasted. This is serious business and God's children should not be diverted from the essential aspects of their spiritual walk and service to become casual and careless about their calling.

Becoming a Profitable Servant

There are three errors you must avoid if you want to become a good steward of God's gifts of grace to you. They are errors so easily made that we do not recognize them.

1. The first is the error of *slothfulness.* It is the error of leaving things unchanged and going on with your life without any change. Sometimes we are plain lazy. Sometimes we just resist change. Whatever the reason, if you don't want to grow then just don't do anything about it.

2. The second error is the error of *disbelief.* Here you say to yourself, "Unless God works a miracle in my life and gives me instant success, fully utilizes all my potential and provides me with the evidence that I am doing it all correctly, I'm not going to begin doing anything myself." You have a long wait ahead of you. It has been my experience that God often wants us to take the first step "in faith." As soon as we move out and trust Him, He confirms our faith and blesses it with assurance. Try it and see for yourself.

3. The third error is the error of *arrogance.* Here you "go it alone." You believe that *all* you need to be successful lies within you. You must just believe in yourself and the power hidden deep within you, and you will be fantastically successful. You believe that like a large reservoir you have hidden depths and unexplored mysteries that only need to be mobilized. You will attempt to rise above your handicaps by yourself. You will set aside your inferiority and create the courage to be self-confident and attain your hopes. Who knows, you may even be successful at doing this. But God won't be a part of it, so it's going to be a lonely trip for you.

I would invite you to avoid these errors and believe with the Apostle Paul, "I can do all things through Christ which strengtheneth me" (Philippians 4:13). I will continue to explore with you the ways in which you can discover your true "gifts of grace" and how you can overcome the forces that would restrict and inhibit you, especially those in your mind.

Paul gives us a very direct answer to all our questing for success, in Romans 12:2:

> And be not conformed to this world: but be ye transformed by the renewing of your *mind,* that ye may prove what is that good, and acceptable, and perfect, will of God (italics added).

It is to the *mind* that we will direct our attention throughout the remainder of this book.

PART TWO
The Mind: God's Gift to You

The next three chapters focus on the mind and how we think. Chapter 5 emphasizes the importance of developing a Christ-like mind. Much of what we experience as spirituality is in the realm of the mind. By controlling how and what we think and disciplining our minds we can free ourselves from neurotic tendencies. Chapter 6 examines the various "styles" of thinking we can engage in. Once we recognize our style, we are well on the way to changing it. Chapter 7 contrasts "crooked" thinking with "straight" thinking. In a simple way, we can become better thinkers. It does not take great intelligence nor is it time-consuming. Paying attention to a few simple rules can help us to be better people.

We cannot live with truth if we cannot discern or establish it for ourselves. Whether we like it or not, life in Christ requires us to be able to think clearly and realistically. If we cannot, we give evil an advantage and habitually become self-defeating and self-degrading.

We are told to "Keep thy heart with all diligence; for out of it are the issues of life" (Proverbs 4:23).

Let us follow this advice.

Disciplining Your Thoughts

Chapter 5

One of the precious gifts God has given us is the mind. It is one of the precious gifts we can give back to Him.

The mind is the center of our being. Whenever Scripture speaks of the *heart,* it usually means the mind. That is why Solomon can say, "For as he thinketh in his heart, so is he" (Proverbs 23:7). Jesus also used the heart as the expression of the mind. In Matthew 15:18 He says, "But those things which proceed out of the mouth come forth from the heart. . . ." Again, in Luke 6:45 He says: "A good man out of the good treasure of his heart bringeth forth that which is good. . . ."

There is no doubt that the mind determines who we are. We are constantly either building or destroying ourselves through the content of our thoughts. To be spiritually and psychologically healthy, therefore, you should at least be able to do the following:

- Control what you think. Thoughts will present themselves randomly to your mind. You will not have chosen these thoughts, but you should be able to control what lingers in your mind. You can learn how to turn away unwanted thoughts.

• Create the content and quality of what fills your mind. In other words, you should be able to build your personality by choosing and generating thoughts that are healthy and wholesome.

• Conduct your logic in a sound and rational manner. The way you think, put ideas together, and draw conclusions from your thinking is vital to your success and happiness.

You can learn to do all of these. They are yours for the choosing. You have sovereign control over your mind and can therefore choose to be who you want to be, or rather who you believe God wants you to be!

The Mind of the Christian

Scripture places great emphasis on the importance of the mind and how we think. Thoughts can be carnal (Romans 8:6), foolish (Proverbs 24:9), full of vanity (Psalms 94:11), evil (Matthew 9:4), spiritual (Romans 8:6), and right (Proverbs 12:5). A mind can be doubting (Luke 12:29) and reprobate (Romans 12:2).

Scripture speaks of the *mind* as signifying different aspects of mental activity. Sometimes the word refers to the conscience whereby we distinguish between good and evil (Titus 1:15). Sometimes it refers to the regenerated part of a person (Romans 7:25), the memory (Psalms 31:12), thought or intention (Isaiah 26:3), the will (1 Peter 5:2), or the affections (Acts 17:11). Taken together, these are all characteristics of the mind.

Most of us don't think much about our mind until something goes wrong with it. What occupies our mind most of every day is ignored. We pay little attention to how we think or the correctness of our conclusions.

Disciplining Your Thoughts

The Christian has a major responsibility to pay attention to the thoughts that are allowed to remain in the mind. We don't allow rats to build nests in our homes, nor do we let grime and dust accumulate to the point where our living is affected. We keep our persons clean with regular physical hygiene. Why should we not give the same attention to the unhealthy thoughts we harbor?

It is in the mind that temptation first occurs. It is here that we lose contact with reality, distort the truth, hold beliefs and attitudes that control us, and that the distortions and inhibiting effects of negative, defeatist thinking take place.

I recently traveled to Holland to teach a stress-management seminar to a group of African evangelists. I decided to stop over in London for a few days before proceeding to Amsterdam. At the end of my stay I left London early in the morning to travel by train to Dover, headed for Brussels. I settled down in my compartment and, feeling a little lonely, began to think about my life situation. I began to replay recent tensions in my work at the seminary and before I realized it, I was quite depressed. Everything seemed hopeless. Everyone seemed to be against me. Nothing seemed to be going right.

Three hours later, while traveling on the boat from Dover to Oostende, I came to my senses and realized that I was allowing my thoughts to distort the truth about my work. I was imagining the worst and exaggerating my petty problems. My thoughts, not the reality of my life, were controlling me. Quickly I straightened out my thinking so that by the time we docked, half an hour later, I had regained my normal emotions.

Such is the power of our thoughts to affect us that I could easily have spent the next few days in quite a depressed state over nothing. An exciting experience traveling by train in a foreign country could have been spoiled.

Starting to Change Your Thoughts

How a Christian thinks is as important as how he or she prays or reads Scripture. Thinking is not free of hazards. Sometimes it is downright inconvenient. It can even be dangerous—if it is not done properly! To be able to discipline the mind is, therefore, something we must learn if we are going to mature.

The disciplining of your thought life can be undertaken as a project that can be combined with your devotional life. Make it a matter of central concern right away. Stop now and ask God to give you the awareness of how your mind works and what you think about that is self-destructive.

Ask Him for power to alter your thoughts and to give you the persistence you will need to discipline your thinking.

Whenever you can, fill your mind with pure and healthy thoughts. Frequently flood your thinking with optimistic and joyful ideas.

Resist reacting to life's blows with defeatist or hopeless thought tendencies. Explore Scripture for the purpose of shaping and changing your values and thought patterns. The thought realm can be a great arena for spiritual growth and sanctification.

Later I will provide you with exercises and helpful suggestions on how to discipline your thoughts. I know that if you work at these you can master your mind and bring it under Christ's control. By sincere and complete trust in God's power this work won't be nearly as hard or demanding as it might at first seem. With God's help you can "short-circuit" much arduous learning and quickly discover that there is help in time of trouble that is fully available to assist you in your task.

How Should a Christian Think?

Scripture is very clear with an answer to this question. The Apostle Paul, in chapter 2 of his letter to the Philippians, verse 5, says: "Let this mind be in you, which was also in Christ Jesus." This is both an injunction and an invitation. Pay careful attention to the word *let*. It places the responsibility for what follows on the reader, on *you!* Paul is, in effect, saying: "You must allow, permit, and make provision for the mind of Christ to be in you." It won't happen unless you allow it to. For Christ's mind to be in you, you must give it complete freedom to control you. Cultivate your mind to receive the thoughts of Jesus. Expect it to be in you and give it the full rein it demands and deserves.

If you open your mind to the thoughts of Christ, you will not be disappointed. Slowly His thoughts will become yours.

How Did Christ Think?

Again, look at Philippians, chapter 2. Christ thought lovingly (verse 2), humbly (verse 3), servingly (verse 7), and obediently (verse 8). His mind was limitless yet He focused it on the reality of His calling and the limitations of His age. He could have thought and claimed great successes, but He remained faithful to His purpose. When tempted by the devil to perform great miracles and claim all the kingdoms of the world as His own, He could not be detracted from His divine purpose by any earthly reward. He kept His mind free of all unholy distraction. His thoughts were centered on the Father's purpose for Him.

Is It Important What a Christian Thinks?

Very! Many Christians erroneously believe that God will miraculously change their personality while they continue to think whatever they like. This won't happen.

A Christ-like character is not a thing of chance. It does not come about miraculously the moment you become a Christian, nor is it given to you without any responsibility on your part to change who you are. It is the natural result of Christ-like thinking—of allowing Christ's thoughts to permeate your mind.

We reap what we sow—in both the physical realm as well as the realm of personality and character. Thoughts are seeds, and the mind is the garden. Keep the weeds away and cultivate the right thoughts and a beautiful garden will grow in the mind.

What Should a Christian Think?

A Christian should always think thoughts that are consistent with what he or she wants to become. Good thoughts can never produce bad results, just as bad thoughts can never produce good results.

A Christian should also think thoughts that will produce the right behaviors. Christ-like behavior begins as a Christ-like thought. Love is first a thought and later becomes a behavior and habit. Grace, peace, kindness, and long-suffering are, first, thoughts God the Holy Spirit plants in your mind; then they emerge as actions. The way you treat your children, serve your employer, or love your spouse will always begin as thoughts.

When Paul, in Philippians 4, verse 8, tells us to "think on" things that are true, honest, just, pure, lovely, of good report, virtuous, and praiseful, he did so because he knew that if we spent time thinking about these qualities of a Christ-like character we would *become* like them. The mind is a factory. Give it the right raw material, and it will produce the right behavior and feelings.

Unfortunately, certain thoughts, like weeds in a garden, are difficult to eradicate. Years of fostering them and savoring their foul characteristics have bred a familiarity that is hard to recognize. Deep within most of our minds are sickly, beastly, impure, and hateful thoughts that have tortuous roots. At times it feels as though these thoughts defy alteration. They are rebellious and perverse.

Take heart, my dear Christian. God knows this and by prayer and the continued filling of your mind with the right thoughts, God will slowly win back your mind to health again.

Controlling Your Thoughts

There are many occasions in the life of all of us when we are bothered by thoughts we don't like or want. These thoughts intrude unnecessarily and no matter how hard we try, we cannot get rid of them. They are unhappy thoughts. They are dirty thoughts. They are hateful, spiteful, revengeful, and revolting thoughts. We don't want them yet they appear as if out of nowhere.

I saw a patient recently who thought he was going out of his mind. Every time he went to church, his mind would fill with the foulest thoughts. He could not believe the filth he would think when trying to worship. What bothered him most was that these thoughts came only when he was in church. In fact, he tried an experiment to see if he could create these thoughts at other times! He couldn't. They only came when he was in church.

He began to wonder whether he was demon possessed. After all, it only happened in church! He prayed for hours for relief—but it never seemed to come. He began to fear going to church because he knew he would be tormented by his uncontrollable mind.

Finally he sought professional help. I reassured him that there was nothing unusual about his experience. It was a form of obsessional thinking and it was quite common. Many Christians go through spells of thinking like this. The fact that it only occurred in church was a function of his guilt and earnest desire to worship sincerely, not the result of any supernatural power's having control over his mind. He was greatly relieved. I taught him some very simple "thought stopping" techniques, which I will describe later in this chapter, and he was quickly able to bring his thinking under control. When last I saw him, he was no longer bothered by unwanted thoughts.

Uncontrolled Thinking

We experience bouts of uncontrollable thinking for many reasons. If you are bothered in this way, review the following points. You may find help from a better understanding of why you do it.

• During periods of intense anxiety our mind engages in persistent, obsessional, and ruminating thinking in an attempt to understand what is making us anxious. Our mind tries to make sense of our crazy world. Rarely does this type of thinking really help. Mostly it only makes us more anxious.

• We try to solve our conflicts by rehearsing past events. We replay encounters with our boss or someone we dislike or are afraid of, hoping that we will find a solution to the conflict. Usually we remember something else that we overlooked and this is more bothersome than the original thought, so that the conflict is intensified rather than resolved.

• We try to anticipate problems that might occur in the near future. We think that if we can imagine all the possible outcomes of an event, we will be better prepared to deal with the future. While some sensible fore-planning is very useful, most of our anticipatory thinking only creates fears about problems that never occur. We live through more crises in our mind than we do in reality, because most of what we anticipate never materializes.

• Bouts of uncontrollable and persistent thinking are often the consequence of disturbed brain chemistry. This can be caused by fatigue, for example, when you are overtired. It can also be brought on by excitement. When you are in this state, you just have to hear a musical tune and it will start playing in your head. The tune will play over and over again, as if you have no control over it.

• Sometimes the disturbance of your brain chemistry is caused by your adrenal glands' being in high gear. When your body has been highly activated, either by an emergency or by a challenging project, you draw on your adrenaline to provide you with reserve energy. Unfortunately, this adrenaline also activates your thinking processes, and your mind will go into high gear. It may keep up the churning activity for some time afterward.

I experience this "adrenal arousal" very often after an evening concert or church meeting. In the case of a concert (sometimes a play) my mind has been aroused to the point of being overactive, and it is very difficult to slow it down to go to sleep. Church meetings, especially if the topics of discussion are very exciting or if some interpersonal conflict has occurred, will also arouse my mind. Sleep is almost impossible afterward. My mind plays and replays the events of the evening until finally, out of sheer exhaustion, it gives up and goes to sleep. This mechanism underlies much chronic insomnia, as many ministers know!

Whatever the mechanism that causes bouts of uncontrollable and very disturbing thinking, it is possible to bring your mind under control. I will now describe some of the techniques used for this purpose.

Thought-Control Techniques

To be able to control your unwanted thoughts whenever you choose is a wonderful blessing—and not very difficult to learn. Persistent thinking that is unproductive and unrealistic is a very common problem encountered in clinical practice. To some extent we all go through periods like this. While it may become chronic and "obsessional" if left untreated for a long time, mostly this thinking occurs during acute periods of stress or fatigue. When the stress is over, the thinking returns to normal.

I will describe four methods by which *thought control* can be achieved: thought stopping; thought redirecting; thought substituting; and thought flooding. Used with prayer and trust in God to deliver you from unwanted thoughts, you should be able to discover a new freedom for your mind. People find that one method works better than another for them. Practice each method until you know it well and then use the one you find the most effective. Of course, you can combine the different methods or alternate their use on different occasions.

1. *Thought Stopping.* This technique has been in clinical use for many years. It begins by asking the patient to practice the blocking on minor and only mildly bothersome thoughts at first. After it is mastered, the technique can be tried on more serious thoughts. Here is what you do:

Lie on your bed in a comfortable position. Select a thought that sometimes bothers you. Take a deep breath and let the air out slowly. Relax every part of your body. Think for a moment about the troublesome thought. Then take the flat of one hand, hit it against your thigh with a sharp and quick slap (but don't hurt yourself) and shout either out loud or in your thinking, "Stop." Relax again. Concentrate on your breathing and the tension in your body. Try to relax any part of the body that feels tense. If the thought comes back into your mind again, repeat the slap and shout the word *stop*. Later, when you have conditioned the word *stop* to the thigh slap, you can just think the word in your mind and it will have the same effect.

It may be helpful if you tape record the instructions given in the preceding paragraph, with appropriate additional suggestions to yourself. You can then play the tape while relaxing and learn the technique more effectively.

Having practiced the slap-and-stop method on minor troublesome thoughts, make a list of others that you are either afraid of or find bothersome. Practice with each one of these thoughts in turn. Then try the technique while going about your regular daily routine. No one else need be aware of what you are doing. While you may have to repeat the exercise eight or ten times on each thought, with practice you will find that thoughts actually stop.

Later you should be able to catch troublesome thoughts at the moment they occur and nip them in the bud. You may say to yourself, "This thought is not going to be helpful. I choose not to let it remain," and then proceed to stop the thought.

2. *Thought Redirecting.* This is a modification of the thought-stopping method, which I have devised to add a component of thought redirection. After you have discovered a thought you don't want and shouted stop to yourself, the old thought may return after a while because nothing else has taken its place. This technique helps to replace the vacuum with an alternative pleasant thought.

For instance, let us suppose you have a work colleague who bothers you. During a coffee break this person says something that hurts you. An hour later you catch yourself rethinking and dwelling on your colleague's words. You can't stop them from playing in your head. Here is how you proceed:

Relax wherever you are, standing or sitting, and think for a moment about the words that are bothering you. Say stop silently to yourself as in the previous exercise, then *immediately* begin to think about your colleague. Think about his office, his desk, and good things you know about him. Think about the positive things he has said to you in the past. Think about his wife and children. Think of your friendship. Think about how human he is—no better than you but also no worse. And so on, and so on . . .

The idea here is to immediately start a chain of thoughts that originate with the bothersome one but which slowly take you away from it to something positive and pleasant. By redirecting your thinking away from the original bothersome thought you continue to occupy your mind with wholesome, healthy, and healing thoughts. The Christian can focus this redirection ultimately on Christ, His love for us, and His glorious salvation. There is always a lot to think about here!

With practice, this technique can become a habit so that you need never allow troublesome thoughts to dominate you.

3. *Thought Substituting.* Thought substitution is a further refinement of the above technique. It differs from thought redirecting in that you deliberately plan ahead of time to have three or four "thought projects" available in your mind to substitute for the troublesome thought.

By thought projects I mean ideas, plans, conquests, or dreams that excite you and can captivate your mind. We all have things we want to do, build, plan, or create. If we begin to think about any one of these exciting projects, they should be able to quickly capture our interest and keep us thinking about them.

To illustrate, let me give you an example of one of my own thought projects. I once learned to fly an airplane. Often, when trying to go to sleep, I will rehearse the flying exercises I had been taught, in my imagination. This is good practice and helps me to remember the complex tasks of flying. It is also an effective way of blocking out unwanted thoughts. Even though I no longer fly, I enjoy doing the exercise. It brings back pleasant memories, as I can spend hours flying in my imagination and enjoy every minute of it. It also doesn't cost me anything!

You can use this technique by making a short list of suitable projects that excite you. It doesn't matter whether they are only imaginary or not. Some examples are designing a dress, planning a vacation, reliving a travel trip, going to the beach or the mountains in your imagination, reciting Scripture, preaching a sermon, writing a book, or creating and telling yourself a story. There is no limit to the thought projects you can invent for your mind.

These projects are then substituted the moment you have said stop to an unwanted thought. You redirect your thinking toward one of these projects and continue to think about them as long as it is necessary to distract yourself from the bothersome thought. If the first thought project you try doesn't do the trick, go to the next. The secret is to have these projects "up your sleeve" and ready to go into action at a moment's notice.

4. *Thought Flooding.* This technique is particularly helpful in dealing with chronic and obsessional types of thought. Obsessional thinking derives its success from the fact that you fear the object of the thought. In other words, you are so afraid of the thought, that when it enters your mind, you immediately try to suppress it. It is this fear and suppression that perpetuates it. The more you try to run away from the thought, the more it will pursue you.

Do you remember playing a childhood game where someone starts chasing you and you run away? The faster they chased you, the faster you ran. After a while you suddenly stop. You turn to your chaser and he stops. Then you start toward him, and he turns and runs away with you now in pursuit.

This is precisely what thought flooding does to obsessional thoughts. It reverses roles. Instead of the thoughts chasing you and you running away and avoiding them, you pursue the thoughts, deliberately and intentionally. They then lose their power over you.

You can use the technique as follows:

Let us suppose you have an obsessional thought you don't want. You realize this and choose to stop it. Think about the troublesome thought for a moment. Say to yourself, "This idea has bothered me for a long time. I am now choosing to deliberately think about it. I will not avoid this thought. I will give it ALL my attention. I will think about nothing else. Now I will think about it. Think now about . . . (substitute your thought here) . . . I will think about nothing else but this. I will keep my mind thinking about it."

Keep up this bombardment of ideas about your troublesome thought as long as possible. After a couple of minutes you will find your mind giving up on the thought and you can then substitute one of your thought projects in its place. If the obsession comes back, repeat the exercise but keep your thinking about the troublesome thought going a little longer.

Obsessional thoughts don't like to be chased. They run away! I know, because I have used the technique very successfully with many of my patients.

Further Help

If, after carefully applying these techniques, you continue to experience chronic, obsessional, and bothersome thoughts, then I would recommend you seek help from a competent counselor, psychologist or psychiatrist. None of us is so thoroughly competent that we can master every technique or be capable of perfect control at all times. Sometimes we need help, and there is nothing to be ashamed of if we seek it from a professional person. Provided you consult a competent professional, preferably one who is understanding of your faith orientation, you have nothing to fear. No matter what the content of your thinking is, you will find in such a person a genuine desire to understand and help you. Such is the nature of troubled thinking that it needs to be dealt with as soon as possible, or else it can become deeply ingrained. With the passing years it becomes more difficult to eradicate.

To be free of troubled thoughts is a blessing. Not to be controlled by the involuntary content of your mind is the foundation of all spiritual and mental health. It is God's gift to us that we can bring our thoughts into harmony with His. His thoughts are not our thoughts since they are so much "higher" than ours (*see* Isaiah 55:8,9). Why not seek to have them with all of your heart? In the next chapter we will examine some of the ways in which your thinking can be out of harmony with God's thinking.

What Kind of Thinker Are You?

When I was thirteen years of age I had a friend. I'll call him Fred. Fred was a very good friend. He was always there when I needed him. My parents had divorced only a year before and I felt very much in need of a consistent and always "ready to help" buddy.

But Fred had one irritating habit. Whenever we were confronted by a situation that seemed hopeless, catastrophic, or just bothersome, he would say, "But don't worry, tomorrow always fixes things." He would then walk away as if the problem no longer existed. Sometimes he was right. Most times he was wrong. "Tomorrow" never solved real problems, only imaginary ones.

We All Think Differently

Fred is typical of many people. He had developed, even at the tender age of thirteen, a particular way or "style" of thinking. This will probably stay with him the rest of his life if he doesn't do something about it. It will shape his personality and determine his successes and failures, just as it will for us.

Is this good? It depends on the style of thinking you adopt. Some thinking patterns can make you. Some can destroy you. Some are in harmony with the way God thinks. Others are so opposite that it is difficult to see how God can bless them.

There are some styles of thinking that *never* produce success. Do you know anyone who is successful who says, "I'll never be able to do it," very often? I don't! What about a person who keeps saying, "But it's impossible. No one has ever done that before"? This person is bound to fail. What about, "Oh, the last time I tried that it didn't work, so why should I bother trying it again"? I cannot believe that such a person ever achieves success, even in minor things.

Your thinking determines who you are and what you can become. God can do nothing with a person whose thinking runs contrary to his basic character.

Examine Your Thinking

As a committed Christian you have a responsibility to constantly examine your thinking. Failure to do this can leave your mind open to all types of influences. It can lead to the undermining of your effectiveness as a vital, dynamic, and influential Christian.

Regular self-examination is highly recommended in Scripture as a profitable and life-changing exercise. Jeremiah, out of his pain over Jerusalem's misery, calls to the people of God, "Let us search and try our ways, and turn again to the Lord" (Lamentations 3:40).

Paul, in his epistle to the Corinthian church, tells them, "Examine yourselves, whether ye be in the faith; prove your own selves. Know ye not your own selves . . ." (2 Corinthians 13:5). This verse is particularly important in emphasizing that we have a responsibility to look at whether we "know ourselves" or not. We cannot ignore important psychological mechanisms within us and expect to have a healthy spirituality.

Central to our psychological functioning is the way we think about the world around us and the behaviors that follow from this thinking. As Christians, we are required to examine this thinking and change it whenever necessary.

Be Willing to Change

Christians should be more willing to change both their thinking and their behavior than non-Christians. After all, they have been given the resources to make change possible, as well as the standards to which they should conform. Unfortunately it is very common to find that Christians believe that God is going to do all the changing for them. They don't have to do anything—God does it all! While God, in Christ, reveals to us what He wants us to be and can through His Spirit help us to see ourselves realistically, He expects us to be obedient and responsive to His prompting and the understanding into ourselves that He gives us. We receive His power to change, but change does not occur without our willingness to participate. God is in a cooperative partnership with us, not a unilateral dictatorship.

This is as true in the realm of our thinking as much as it is in other aspects of our walk with God.

Neurotic Styles of Thinking

Some styles of thinking are downright bad. They are neurotic in the sense that they upset our emotional balance and disturb our spiritual composure. They produce fairly predictable effects. The rules of destruction are simple to understand and the outcome predictable.

Shakespeare, in *The Merry Wives of Windsor*, has Mrs. Ford say to one of the gentlemen living at Windsor, "Heaven make you better than your thoughts!"

What a beautiful idea! How liberating for the Christian. This should be our prayer: that God will take and mold us so that we will not be just what we think, but better.

There are many neurotic ways of thinking that can sabotage or defeat us. I will discuss some in the hope that you will discover the style you use—then leave you with a choice. You can continue to think this way, or you can change. The first step in all change is the recognition that you need to change. Once you admit this, you are well on the way toward changing. So be honest in evaluating yourself and willing to admit your errors.

The styles of thinking I will discuss do not occur singularly in any one person. We can all have more than one of these styles working within us at one time. We may operate in one way at one time and then change to another at some other time. As you prayerfully read the description of each, examine the way you think. Ask God to help you identify yourself. Do not be unduly self-critical and don't condemn yourself for what you discover. Be thankful for the insight to change. Self-condemnation seldom leads to constructive change, only to more guilt and depression!

1. NEGATIVE THINKING

This style is very common in our success-oriented culture. As a general category of thinking it uses a number of strategies to make the thinker unhappy, pessimistic, and defeated. Of all the styles of thinking it causes the most misery and failure.

The world is full of negative thinkers. They are all around us. Charles Schulz, the creator of the Peanuts cartoons, presents many incidents that show us what it is like to be this way. Of all his characters, Lucy must surely be the most negative. Her basic personality overflows with everything negative and crabby. While on the outside she appears optimistic, she can easily see the worst in anything. She can predict the most dire consequences. And, if called upon, she can dispense all the necessary punishment anyone may need to feel terrible. There's probably a little of Lucy in all of us—which is what Schulz is trying to say through his cartoons.

In one cartoon Lucy is standing talking to Linus, who is clutching his security blanket and sucking his thumb.

"I'm going to tell you something I've never told anyone before," she says. "Do you see that hill over there? Someday I'm going to go over that hill and find the answer to my dreams . . . Someday I'm going to go over that hill and find happiness and fulfillment. I think for me, ALL the answers to life lie beyond those clouds and over the grassy slope of THAT hill!"

Linus looks up, takes his thumb out of his mouth, and says: "Perhaps there's another little kid on the other side of that hill, who is looking this way and thinking that all the answers to life lie on this side of that hill."

Lucy pauses for a moment, looks at Linus, then looks at the hill, and screams, "FORGET IT, KID!"*

Many books have been written about negative thinking, so most people have some idea of how this style operates. However, in my review of the more popular books on this subject, I have not encountered a clear statement of what it is or how it comes about. So let me try to summarize what I see are its main characteristics.

There are three emotional factors that contribute to negative thinking: fear, anger, and depression.

Fear lies behind much negativity. Such conditioning occurs very early in life, usually through rejection by others. Parents who are extremely conditional in the love they give their children often create this fear. They only show their love when their children are obedient. When their child disobeys or displeases them, they withdraw their love as punishment for the misdeed or deviation. Need I say that this form of punishment is extremely cruel? It can turn a hopeful, optimistic child into a negative, fear-ridden adult who is too afraid to risk buying a new style of shoe or ask for a well-deserved promotion. Such people always believe that they will be punished for being different.

Anger is also a major cause of negativity. The anger is first formed in response to early hurts or shameful experiences. Parents who label children as "hopeless," or who keep saying, "You'll never amount to anything," or who use verbal abuse that degrades their child, can lay the foundation for this anger. Since the child cannot direct the anger back at the parent, it is sup-

---

* Text from PEANUTS by Charles M. Schulz; © 1968 by United Feature Syndicate, Inc.

pressed. Like a hidden cancer it then does its damage throughout the whole personality. I have known it to prevent a full commitment even to God. God becomes the scapegoat on whom the anger is vented in open or unconscious ways. Even He cannot be trusted.

This suppressed anger often causes the development of what we call the *passive-aggressive personality*. Such a person expresses anger in indirect or passive ways. A teenager, for instance, may resist doing chores or persist in failing school even though he is extremely intelligent. The anger is vented by punishing the parents or other significant persons by not giving them what they want. Unfortunately the child also suffers from this behavior because he or she also does not get what they want.

Suppressed anger can also lead to negative thinking. A self-statement like "I'm no good for the job, so I won't even apply for it" is as much an expression of hostility toward the self and other loved ones as it is a negative-thinking style. "I don't believe I can understand this subject, so I won't even open the book and start studying" is negative thinking, but it can also be an unrecognized and unexpressed internal rage. Only deep Christian-oriented psychotherapy can bring healing to such intense rage.

Depression can also lead to negative thinking. One of the major symptoms of depression is a loss of all interest in life. Ambition goes away and hope is muzzled. Negative thinking here finds a ready soil in which to grow. Depression causes everything to seem dark and threatening.

Fortunately, the negative thinking of depression lasts only as long as the depression itself in most instances. As soon as the depression lifts, so do the "I can'ts, I won'ts, and what's the use's."

Negative thinking always sees and exaggerates minor problems. It is harmful to the soul because it distorts reality and sabotages all potential. One gives up without trying and surrenders without a fight.

I recall that as a very small boy I was required to run a race at our Sunday School picnic. Most of the other boys my age seemed larger, so when we were lined up to start the race, with one mother holding a handkerchief as a starting flag and two mothers holding a piece of string as the finishing line, my heart sank! I believed I could never run such a race and win. Everyone was bigger than me. It was hopeless. When the handkerchief dropped, I made a half-hearted attempt to start, then bluffed that my ankle hurt, and limped to the sideline.

That got me out of the races for the rest of the day, but when they later handed out the prizes, and I saw that all the boys who simply finished a race got a brand-new pocketknife, I was devastated. How foolish of me! Winning wasn't the point at all; it was sufficient just to cross the finishing line in order to win a prize. There were no firsts or seconds, just race completers.

Years later when I became a Christian and encountered those portions of Scripture that compared the Christian life to a footrace, I knew exactly what was meant. For example, in the verse "... let us run with patience the race that is set before us" (Hebrews 12:1), patience is the endurance factor. All you have to do is *finish* the race, you don't have to *win*. Negative thinkers don't endure; they hardly ever start and when they do, they quickly drop out of the race.

Perhaps the greatest example of negative thinking I have ever encountered is told in Numbers 13. You will remember that when the children of Israel arrived on the edge of Canaan and were to go in and possess it, God invited Moses to send spies and search out the land that He had given them. One man from each tribe was selected and sent to see the land, its people, its dwellings, and to bring back a sample of its fruit.

When the spies returned, they reported that the land overflowed with milk and honey. It was a wonderful land. But, and it was a big BUT, there were a lot of people to overcome. One of the spies, Caleb, having the strength of these people and God's power, says, "Let us go up at once, and possess it; for we are well able to overcome it" (verse 30).

But he was a lonely voice! The other eleven spies were negative thinkers. They didn't believe in the power of God. Verse 33 should be painted in large letters and hung on the living-room wall of every negative thinker, because it so adequately captures the essence of their thinking:

"THERE WE SAW THE GIANTS ... AND WE WERE ... AS GRASSHOPPERS...."

Even if it were true, it was a lie! Paradoxical? Not really. It did not take God into account. It reckoned only with obstacles and not with the resources they had on their side.

Everyone wept that night, and so they should have. Every last one of them would die before their offspring could claim the land of Canaan as their inheritance from God.

I fear that many of us, in our negative moments if not in every aspect of our life, believe the reports of our "internal" spies. They always use negative thinking. We see giants when we should be seeing victory. We see ourselves as grasshoppers when we should be seeing strength. We see defeat when we should be sharpening our swords. We see hopelessness when we should be putting on the whole armor of God.

Is it any wonder that we hardly ever succeed at anything we attempt, or that we never attempt anything significant and therefore never succeed?

2. WISHFUL THINKING

Wishful thinkers sometimes believe that they are the opposite of negative thinkers—but they are not. This type of thinking deludes us into believing we are OK, when in fact we are not! It appears on the surface to be healthy, but it can be as ineffective and self-destructive as negative thinking.

Wishful thinkers daydream a lot. They tend to solve problems not by taking direct control and dealing constructively with the issues before them but through fantasy. They resolve conflicts in their imagination and not in real life. They spend wasteful hours thinking about events or encounters with people and in their imagination try to solve some issue, relive an experience, or respond differently to some put-down. Seldom do these fantasized reactions get translated into real-life action. They remain dreams. The next time they get hurt, they again fail to take control, just as in the past.

Daydreaming is helpful when you have nothing to do. On those warm, relaxing afternoons when you sunbathe at the beach or local swimming pool, or when you are traveling a long distance in a bus or airplane and must kill time, you can daydream. It is pleasant when it is used to relive a happy experience or recapture a poignant moment. It can even be therapeutic. Daydreaming provides distraction and release from the stress-producing demands of a hectic life. But it has no place as a thinking style in the successful person's mind. It does not solve problems, it only rehearses them. It does not reduce anxiety, it only generates more.

Wishful thinkers hope a lot. I do not mean that they are full of hope—that is something different. I mean they "wish" that things would change, a lot. They even pray their wishes and expect God to change things, a lot! They have difficulty accepting unchangeable circumstances. They want the impossible to happen and wish that God would make things over for them.

I went through a period in my late teens when I resented some aspects of my life. I desperately wanted to be a taller, stronger, handsomer young man and, especially, more attractive to girls. I even prayed that God would "fix me up" while I slept and that I would wake up in the morning all new and shining. It sounds ridiculous as I recount it now, but I did not like reality very much at that stage of my life, and wishful thinking gave me a way of escaping.

I soon discovered that it brought only temporary relief. Next morning it was gone. Reality kept showing up in the mirror, and no matter how hard I wished for a change, it just didn't happen. If I accepted the unchangeable I would be a lot happier, I finally decided.

I also wanted to be richer. The years I spent preparing for my professional career were lean years. Every cent had to be budgeted, and money took on an exaggerated importance. I wished I could discover a hidden treasure, stumble across some extremely rare coin, or that my grandparents would give me my inheritance ahead of time. I knew there wasn't much to expect from such an inheritance, but wishful thinkers don't bother with reality, anyway.

I dreamed of winning a fabulous lottery (although I never did buy a lottery ticket) or that some long-forgotten distant relative would appear and offer me part of his fortune (I think I saw this idea in a movie or read it in a book). But none of my wishes ever came true. I've had to work hard for everything I've accomplished, and I'm not sorry.

Wishful thinkers often fail to grow up. They like fairy stories and happy endings and they dislike funerals. They tend to idealize life and people and romanticize all human experiences. They want life to present them only with pleasant and sunny days. Dark and cloudy moments are avoided and when they are finally trapped by more trouble than they can handle, they merely escape into more wishful thinking.

Wishful thinkers seldom take action before a catastrophe strikes. Even when they see it coming they are not action oriented but tend toward helplessness. It is especially when they know they are heading for disaster that they throw up their hands and begin wishing rather than planning, hoping rather than claiming, and running away instead of confronting their problems. Many so-called positive thinkers are only wishful thinkers at heart. They've been deluded into believing that things change just because you think positively. Who neglected to tell them that hard work was also a part of the deal for success?

3. WORRY THINKING

Worry thinkers have always been around. I remember encountering them even when I was only a little boy. Jesus encountered many and had to tell them, "Let not your heart be troubled: ye believe in God, believe also in me" (John 14:1).

Paul also admonished his readers, "Don't worry about anything" (Philippians 4:6 TLB), and Peter had to remind his readers,

"Casting all your care upon him, for he careth for you" (1 Peter 5:7).

The tendency to worry is built into all of us. It is partly a biochemical function, in that the brain generates the worry to protect us from harm. Our brain comprises complex chemicals that become disturbed whenever we are threatened. Whether the threat is real or just imagined, we sometimes cannot avoid the "worry mode" of thinking. It is partly a function of our fallen nature and the consequence of living in a sinful and unpredictable world.

Sometimes worrying is helpful, but not very often. It can force us to change our mind or take some constructive steps to remove a threat. Most times worrying is unnecessary, useless, wasteful, and self-destructive. Sometimes we have to worry. Our body forces our mind to become anxious because action is needed. Usually, worry is pointless.

Just recently I lay awake half the night thinking about three interviews I had to conduct the next day. One was with a member of my faculty, another was with a graduate student in our program, and a third was with an administrator of one of our clinics. They had all asked for interviews with me. As dean I was duty bound to meet with them and hear what they had to say.

As I lay thinking about the next day's events, I asked myself all sorts of questions. What did they want to talk about? Were they troubled by something I had said or done? Were they going to resign and leave me in the lurch? Why was I so stupid as to set up interviews when I did not know what we were going to talk about? I was in a worry mode. Hours slipped by and sleep would not come. Finally I reasoned to myself that I was worrying for nothing. What I feared probably would not come to pass. I decided I would play a game with myself. I reached for a pen and pad and jotted down every possible issue I feared would be discussed the next day. I came up with a list of seven items. Deep down I knew I was exaggerating my fears, but I wanted to see just how much my imagination was influencing my thinking. Finally I fell asleep.

At the end of the next day I retrieved my list of "worry issues" and could not believe my eyes. Not a single issue I had feared and listed had come up. In fact, most of the seven items seemed quite ridiculous in the light and sanity of the next day!

Worry thinkers like to make mountains out of molehills. They can take little thoughts and minor fears and turn them into horrendous catastrophes. Johnny may come home from the dentist with three cavities but worry-thinking moms can use that information to turn kids into toothless monsters. Worry-thinking dads can turn a C grade in math on Johnny's latest report card into disaster and poverty.

Worry thinkers enjoy worrying. Don't let them convince you otherwise! They revel in things to worry over and catastrophes to plan, and they don't always want to change this. Life's pleasures are not fulfilled without many hours spent in pointless ponderings over the many ways things can go wrong. You can become so accustomed to worrying that when you no longer have anything to worry about, you feel quite anxious!

Worry thinkers like to worry about everything. It is not enough just to worry about one real issue. They want to include everything. Violet comes upon Charlie Brown and Linus one day, who are both looking frightened. She asks them, "What are you two looking so worried about?" Charlie Brown answers, "We're afraid of the future!"

Violet thinks for a moment, then asks, "Well, are you afraid of tomorrow? Friday? Next week? Anything in particular?"

"No," replies Linus, taking his thumb out of his mouth, "We're worried about EVERYTHING! Yes, our worrying is very broad-minded!"*

That just about captures it for most worriers.

Worry thinkers also love to give forewarnings. They consistently sound the alarm and give dire predictions of doom because it makes them feel better. If you are going on a trip, they tell you to be careful because the accident statistics have shown an increase recently or because the quality of rubber in tires is not

---

* Text from PEANUTS by Charles M. Schulz; © 1959 United Feature Syndicate, Inc.

what it used to be. If you borrow a garden tool, they must warn you not to leave it out in the rain. If you buy a new automobile, they predict that the manufacturer will go out of business or that the price is going to drop. The worry thinker believes that these predictions of doom will help to keep the doom from materializing. "If you worry about it, it doesn't happen," one nine-year-old child told me once, thus completing my psychological training for me! I know many adults who believe this too.

Worry thinkers want others to worry also. They feel most uncomfortable when no one else worries with them. They resent people who are calm and peaceful. They especially dislike people who are positive and optimistic, because these people usually have good arguments for not worrying.

Worry thinkers love to panic. They enjoy the thrill of hysterical shouting and the panic of disaster. They rush hither and thither, savoring every morsel of mischief, and make a great show of their predictions that doom is about to descend. If it doesn't, they are very depressed for weeks afterward.

Worry thinkers don't like it when things go smoothly. They need occasional evidence that trouble is something real so as to keep their hopes of doom up. Something must go wrong occasionally to prove they are right. They welcome the occasional rejection, flat tire, speeding ticket, especially when the spouse gets it. Once in a while a flood is useful, also. If nothing goes wrong for a long time, they feel very uncomfortable.

Charles Schulz has drawn a wonderful Charlie Brown cartoon about how worry thinkers operate. In it Lucy is watching Snoopy dancing around ecstatically happy. She can't stand his happiness so she says, "Happiness isn't everything, Snoopy."

He continues dancing.

"Happiness won't bring you peace of mind," she continues.

Still Snoopy dances.

"My great-grandmother used to say, 'If you're too happy today, you'll only be more unhappy tomorrow.'"

But Snoopy continues to dance.

Finally Lucy runs forward, grabs Snoopy by the throat and

says, "Are you trying to make a fool out of my great-grand-mother?"*

Worry thinkers like to be prepared for the worst. They must never let their guard down lest disaster come upon them unawares. They might miss a wonderful opportunity to be miserable.

4.   SLOB THINKING

People who are very careless in their logic and who cannot reason clearly or rationally, I call "slob thinkers." In the physical world a slob is anyone who is slovenly and habitually untidy. Shoelaces are always left untied, clothes are always disorganized, and hair unkempt. Some people are like this in their thinking. Thoughts and ideas lie scattered around their mind in disarray. They are never "picked up" or arranged in their proper place. Consequently they can't think clearly and their reasoning is hopeless. Needless to say, slob thinkers go through life experiencing much emotional pain and unhappiness, also.

Slob thinking is a bad habit. You learn it and then you keep on doing it. Slob thinkers don't like thinking in the first place. They prefer the right things to happen to them without effort. Thinking means they've got to clear up their mind and put ideas back where they belong, and they don't like doing this.

Geof is my favorite slob thinker. I became friends with him in my early twenties, though I had known him for a number of years.

Geof always got into trouble. Not because he was stupid. He wasn't. But because he was a slob thinker. He would buy a used car and within a week the bottom would fall out of the engine. When asked why he did not have it checked before he bought it, he would reply, "But the fellow who sold it to me said I didn't have to worry. His cousin had looked it over and it was in A1 condition."

One day Geof bought a small powerboat. He invited me to go

---

* Text from PEANUTS by Charles M. Schulz; © 1956 United Feature Syndicate, Inc.

out on the ocean for a "test drive" with him. Together we struggled to get the boat in the water. Geof got the motor started and we set off for a trip. He headed straight out to sea. I asked him, "How much gas do you have?" "Plenty," he replied. "Did you check the tank yourself?" I asked. Just then the engine sputtered. It was a long paddle back to the dock, just using our hands! A few weeks later he asked me if I wanted to learn to fly an airplane with him. I declined!

Slob thinkers think that everything is plain common sense. Everything is obvious and nothing needs to be pondered over or reasoned correctly. In fact, they don't have to think at all. Common sense guides their workaday existence. Common sense dictates all the important decisions even if the issues are profound and very complex. When you ask a slob thinker what he means by common sense he usually replies, "Oh, I don't know, it's just the first thing that comes to my mind."

Slob thinkers never take time to be critical or reflective. This takes too much out of them. They make decisions in a flash— even though they've been wrong 95 percent of the time.

Slob thinkers tend to let their emotions make their decisions. They "feel" a lot and know whether something is right or wrong "in their guts." They don't like to be bothered with facts because these only confuse them. Once they've made up their mind about an issue they never change it. "Decisions are decisions and you've got to stick by them no matter what" is their motto!

Slob thinkers jump to the wrong conclusion a good deal of the time. They see one sow bug and they conclude that the whole garden is infested with them. Daughter may come home late from a date once, and she's "on the road to degradation."

Slob thinkers also overgeneralize a lot. They get bad service from one waiter in a restaurant, and the restaurant is forever damned. If it happens a little bit, then it must happen a lot is the way they reason. Consequently, they miss much in life.

Needless to say, slob thinkers make many wrong decisions. Since they cannot put ideas together correctly or reason through anything but the simplest of problems, they are bound to come to wrong conclusions. This is why trouble dogs them so much. Do

you know the sort of person I am referring to? Trouble stalks
them everywhere. They invest in exotic land in a distant holiday
center and discover the land is in a swamp. They decide to
change jobs, and their new employer goes out of business one
month later.

Everything seems to go wrong. Is the problem simply one of
bad luck? I don't believe there is such a thing as "luck," so I
doubt if this is the explanation. No, it is a matter of not taking
the trouble to use their reasoning ability. People who always experience trouble are people who make wrong decisions because
they don't think. They don't look clearly enough at reality. They
miss the essential data or overlook potential danger and consequently always come out on the wrong side of a decision.

5. REALITY THINKING

By contrast with the other styles of thinking, the reality thinker
embraces everything positive, healthy, and creative he or she
knows about our world. Recognizing the limitations of the
human mind and how easily it can be distorted, this person lives
in complete trust that God will guide, mold, shape, change, and
direct his or her mind, yet is able to think clearly about what is
happening.

Reality thinkers keep an open mind, observing, analyzing,
questioning, and then carefully considering all the facts before
making major decisions.

Reality thinking draws on both objective and subjective data.
It does not ignore feelings, but it does carefully evaluate them. It
asks, "Am I feeling this way because my mind has data I am not
consciously aware of, or am I reacting emotionally without real
cause?" I have often felt strongly about something without being
able to verbalize why I feel the way I do. I will say, "I can't give a
reason why, but I really do believe that this is the wrong decision." Sometimes this feeling has been God's leading. Sometimes
it has been an intuitive reaction. Whatever the reason, I have
learned to pay strict attention to these feelings and to weigh them
very carefully before making a decision.

There are no easy rules I can give to guide you except to say that if you regularly make wrong decisions based on your feelings, then don't trust these feelings. God understands and will find another way to guide you.

Reality thinking approaches problems both intuitively and logically. It is possible to be too rational. You can be so clever in your reasoning that you think yourself into a mire of conflicting, ambiguous, and unresolvable ideas. You can get bogged down by so many "ifs," "buts," and "on the other hand's," that you never make a decision. Reality thinking recognizes that you can't know everything, and sometimes you must make decisions based on "intuition." But intuition is different from "feeling." Intuition has a wisdom about it, born of years of experience in making both right and wrong decisions. It is an instinctive knowledge or a wisdom that comes only from careful attention to how you think. It can provide a shortcut in reasoning.

Most successful people have this intuition. They instinctively know when something is right or wrong and don't waste time debating the instinct. They cannot explain it, let alone describe it. Often they have feelings that run contrary to their intuition, but they trust the wisdom of their intuition over their feelings.

How can you develop this type of intuitive ability to think? There are no simple rules. Only people with the courage to risk making decisions ever learn it, because it comes with experience. It doesn't take a particular type of intelligence, or much intelligence at all for that matter. I have known wise people who don't know any algebra and could not spell *conjugate,* let alone do it. But they have been so "wise" that I have often sought their counsel when my own thinking has been confused.

I also know this: God has placed at our disposal a great store of wisdom in Christ ("In whom are hid all the treasures of wisdom and knowledge" Colossians 2:3), and this wisdom is ours for the asking. "If any of you lack wisdom, let him ask of God, that giveth to all men liberally . . . and it shall be given him" (James 1:5).

The real glory of this wisdom is that it is "perfect." It knows what we really need and responds to this rather than to what we want. To ask for this wisdom so that you may be rich and famous may be to ask for what you really don't need. To live out this wisdom is to guarantee that you will be a whole person.

Receiving God's Wisdom

These, then, are some of the styles of thinking we may adopt. Some are healthy, others are not. I have tried to stress that in order to receive God's wisdom, we must learn how to think, and how to think correctly. If we don't, we cannot really use the wisdom God gives us.

Thinking correctly is *not* a matter of intelligence, just as genuine wisdom is not. It is more a matter of "thinking straight." It is the following after truth and the application of this truth to our life in Christ. In the next chapter we will explore in more detail what it is to think straight.

The Art of Thinking Straight

Chapter 7

Success is not a trivial matter. It brings with it tremendous responsibilities. It is also not a once-only phenomenon. If you are successful, you have to keep on being successful or else you lose it. It's like a merry-go-round. Once you're on it you have to stay on it! Furthermore, managing a successful life takes a commitment of time, energy, and courage, and not many people have one, let alone all three of these abilities.

While an opportunity to become successful may present itself to many quite by chance, few are able to rise to the challenge and grasp it, because their thinking is not prepared for it. They may have a wonderful opportunity within their grasp to do something really meaningful with their life, and they will sit staring at it, wondering whether or not to take the risk. Because they hesitate, it slips through their fingers into oblivion.

Correct thinking is essential to maintaining a holistically successful life. This is true whether the success has to do with having a happy marriage, being content in your job, or enjoying your recreation hours. For the Christian, the understanding of Scripture also requires clear thinking. Even praying, no matter how childlike and simple, requires some thinking. You cannot avoid using your mind if you want to live.

Thomas Edison was a successful man. His inventive genius gave us the electric light bulb, the phonograph, the motion picture camera, and a host of other benefits. But his success was not just a matter of knowing how to use the right tools or be a wizard with gadgets. He was a very careful thinker. He thought a lot. He did this thinking deliberately. No detail was too small to escape his attention and no job was too menial or petty for him to perform. He would often say, "My business is thinking." On the wall of every room at his Menlo Park headquarters was a quotation from the British artist Sir Joshua Reynolds. It read, "There is no expedient to which a man will not resort to avoid the real labor of thinking." He made sure he thought a lot—and it made him successful.

Thinking Crookedly

But what if you can think, and spend a lot of time thinking, but your thinking gets you nowhere? You spend hours ruminating over issues but you never solve any problems. The chances are that you have developed a "crooked thinking" syndrome.

Humans have a natural tendency to think crookedly. It doesn't take any effort and it requires no training. It just happens! This is why simply changing to positive thinking is not enough. If you think crookedly, positive thinking is just going to get you into more trouble. While reality thinking is always thinking positively, it is also straight and clear thinking. When you bring them all together you have a powerful combination.

The best analogy I can think of is the engine in your motor car. It may idle roughly and be very erratic when you press down on the accelerator (negative thinking). You clean out the carburetor and tune the ignition until it has fantastic power and speed (positive thinking). But what do you do with it now? Crooked positive

thinking is like having a powerful and well-tuned engine but
with the steering wheel disconnected from the front wheels of the
car. You have no control over your power, so your car goes
around in circles or in a direction you don't want it to go. Positive thinking, when it is not connected to clear, rational, and realistic thinking, will get you where you don't want to go, very fast!

One young businessman I counseled with was just like this.
Every idea, project, and business scheme sounded great to him.
He received everything positively and seldom used his critical
thinking to screen out harebrained schemes. He was a sucker for
con artists. He could be convinced that every gadget and inven-
tion was the greatest idea ever thought of. Over a five-year period he wasted every cent of a fairly large inheritance because he
received everything positively, believed positively, acted positively, and positively failed because he could not keep his feet on
the ground. He was convinced, quite literally, that if you *really*
believed in something, you could make it work. It took many
hours of therapy to convince him that positive thinking was only
one of the ingredients of success. You also have to have a good
idea.

Crooked thinking is self-defeating thinking. It works against
you. One popular teacher of positive-thinking skills in the business world calls crooked thinking "stinkin' thinkin' " and that is
what it is. It stinks, presumably, because it fouls up your own
nest.

The crooked thinking so often encountered in Christian circles
is not the fault of the Gospel. I believe that everything about our
Christian faith is healthy and productive of a sound mind, strong
ego, and wholesome personality. But not every Christian group is
healthy, I am sorry to say. Some spawn emotionally conflicted
and neurotic personalities, primarily, through the way they teach
their followers to think. Often the message is "let us (the leaders)
do the thinking for you. You just do what we tell you to do."

Jim Jones was a master at this and he took control of his followers by taking over responsibility for their thinking. Unfortunately, we have many minor Jim Joneses around who also

control people's minds. While they are not likely to lead their flock to physical self-destruction as Jim Jones did, they are nevertheless taking many down the road to psychological and spiritual self-destruction. People, as a whole, are easily influenced and prefer others to do their thinking for them. To be successful you must do your own thinking.

The Signs of Crooked Thinking

What are the ways in which thinking can be "crooked"? Let me reassure you that I am not asking you to engage in complicated or overintelligent thinking when I stress the need for straight thinking. Crooked thinking is crooked in very simple ways. Straighten out these simple kinks and you can begin to improve many aspects of your life. Pay attention to a few simple rules and your positive thinking will take you in whatever direction you choose to go.

Here are some signs of crooked thinking:

Crooked thinking is *gullible* thinking. You will believe almost anything you are told. You receive information or ideas and uncritically make them your own. You never question anyone's point of view. You believe everyone else is an expert and you are simply a learner.

This thinking lets other people predigest your beliefs. They say "now believe this"—and you do! It is characteristic of early-childhood thinking. Obviously, when we first become aware of the world around us as little children, we are very dependent on our parents and siblings for our information and the data for our beliefs. We believe what they tell us. We never question whether it is right or wrong. If we continue to think this way into adulthood then we can expect to get into trouble—with others and with our emotions. As we grow, we have to learn to think for ourselves.

Have you ever played a game with someone who believes anything you tell him or her? It's cruel and somewhat demeaning, but I suppose we've all done it. Poor Paul. He was in our fifth-grade class. He believed anything anyone told him. "The principal wants to see you, Paul," someone would say. And, dutifully, Paul would trot off to the principal's office only to be embarrassed—not once, but many times. Or, "I just heard from Bill that the teacher doesn't want us to do any homework today." Paul would smile and say, "That's great," never question whether he was having his leg pulled or not, and be in serious trouble at school the next day.

Once we told Paul he had been hypnotized by the boy behind him and he couldn't move his leg. He believed us and sat in his seat for a long time before someone told him we were only "pulling his leg."

Now, lest you claim you are not this gullible, why don't you take a moment to reflect on how much you believe simply because someone else told you to believe it? Think about your habits, dress, ideas, plans, goals, and accomplishments. Are these really yours? Perhaps they started out as coming from someone else, but have you thought them through so you now know you want them for yourself?

Charles Schulz drew a cartoon once that showed Charlie Brown coming upon Lucy watering the lawn. The cartoon shows Lucy holding the hose, sprinkling water all over the grass and shouting, "It's raining, it's raining! The clouds are opening and the rain is falling!"

Charlie Brown walks up behind her and she continues shouting, "It's raining, it's pouring, the rain is falling." Then she turns to Charlie Brown and with a big grin says, "Grass will believe anything you tell it!"*

The person who cannot critically evaluate what he or she hears and carefully determine its accuracy and decide for themselves what they will believe seldom has the freedom to become successful.

First John 4, verse 1, emphasizes this point. We are told, "Beloved, believe not every spirit, but try the spirits whether they are of God. . . ." The Living Bible translates it this way, "Dearly loved friends, don't always believe everything you hear just be-

---

* Text from PEANUTS by Charles M. Schulz; © 1975 United Feature Syndicate, Inc.

cause someone says it is a message from God: test it first to see if it really is."

I am not saying that you should become a skeptic. Skeptics are quite impossible to live and work with. They question everything just for the fun of being impossible. Skeptics don't really want to know the truth. They just want to be difficult and draw attention to themselves. They are argumentative. They play devil's advocate just for their personal gratification and glorification. The Apostle John is not advocating this.

Avoid skepticism like the plague! It is a form of negative thinking. No thoroughbred skeptic has ever become really successful. They even have trouble believing that the Gospel is true because they want "tangible proof" about everything.

But then, so did the children of Israel. When they were on their way from Egypt to the promised land and became discouraged, they stopped believing and started doubting. God would then give them a sign to restore their faith, but such is the nature of the human mind that they soon forgot it. With Pharaoh hot in pursuit they came to the Red Sea, thought they were doomed, but God parted the sea for them. When they were starving in the desert and complained, God gave them manna. When they were thirsty and the water of Marah was as bitter as their hearts, God gave them a tree that made the water sweet. When they were tired of manna and complained about the monotony of their food, God sent them quail. And still they complained and wanted proof that God was with them! The more proof God gave them the more they wanted and the shorter their memories of His faithfulness became.

Dearly beloved, this is *our* nature also. Human skepticism in the spiritual realm can never be satisfied with "proofs." Faith is a gift to be received and cherished with all one's heart.

Crooked Thinking Is Prejudiced Thinking

When Jeremiah said, "The heart is deceitful above all things ... who can know it?" (Jeremiah 17:9), he was really talking about the mind. The mind of the crooked thinker can also be prejudiced above all things. Here the mind tends not to be open to new ideas or to being altered very easily. When it believes something, it wants to go on believing it even when there is evidence to the contrary.

This is what maintains much racial prejudice. You learn it when you are young and then do not want to change it later. If you can choose between believing the best about someone and believing the worst, which do you think the crooked thinker would believe? I recall that not too long ago a rumor circulated about the marriage breakup of a prominent Christian leader. There was absolutely no truth to the rumor. It was a case of mistaken identity. The newspaper had given a name identical to that of the prominent leader and described how a sordid divorce had taken place. Many people grabbed at the story, savored, and delighted in it like a crowd of vultures devouring a carcass. It is as if they enjoyed "catching" someone in sin. Such is the tendency of prejudiced thinking.

Prejudiced thinking is not open to new ideas. It wants to hang on to the old. It is afraid of new ideas, not because they are novel, but because they trigger some deep-seated insecurity. The status quo must be maintained at all costs. This guarantees comfort. But this also cuts these thinkers off from true creativity. To be truly creative one must be free to think new ideas and find new ways of doing things. Prejudice will insist that there is only one way to do things, but this will stifle success. Holistically successful people are not prejudiced thinkers.

Prejudiced thinking is also prejudged thinking. Since everything is prejudged, no real effort need go into thinking anyway! "I know ahead of time how the issue will turn out, so I don't even bother to think about it" is the typical crooked-thinker's motto.

To prejudge is to make up your mind ahead of time how you feel about something. Prejudgment reduces flexibility and openness to how things really are. A tendency to use prejudgment is found in people who dislike making decisions. They find it hard to choose one way over another. If they select green they worry,

"Isn't blue better?" The dreadful feeling that they may have made a wrong decision makes it painful for them to live by it. Every day brings a new worry. The constant feeling that one has made a mistake is often worse than any consequence of a wrong decision. So to avoid this torment these people make all kinds of rules and generalizations to cover every aspect of their living. The rules help them to avoid decision making. Look at some of these rules:

"I can't go out on Tuesday evenings because that is when I need to wash my hair."

"I can't plan a holiday next year because I never know when something unexpected will come up."

"I can't set a goal for this project because whenever I set goals I'm disappointed."

This person lives by rules—rules carefully constructed to avoid making decisions. If you always do something one way, then continuing to do it that way guarantees personal comfort. It also guarantees nonsuccess!

Unfortunately life doesn't fit into "rule boxes." Decisions often have to be made where there is no previous experience to guide you. Failure to make any decision (because you have a rule for that) is in fact making a decision. It is a decision not to do something.

All successful people are good decision makers. They don't jump to quick decisions, but they make them after very carefully weighing all the data. Prejudiced thinkers either avoid making decisions or they make them impulsively and without carefully evaluating the data.

Crooked Thinkers Are Assumptive Thinkers

Crooked thinkers make a great many assumptions without realizing it.

We take a lot for granted, don't we? When I drive on the freeway, I assume that everyone else will obey the same rules that I do. I assume they'll stay in their lane, signal if they want to change lanes, and not suddenly stop. These assumptions are reasonable and we all take them for granted. They provide safety. They are warranted because there are laws that govern them and driving tests that guarantee them—at least to a reasonable level of performance.

But crooked thinkers don't stop here. They believe that assumptions can be made about almost everything, even when there are no laws.

For instance, these thinkers assume that everyone sees things as they do. Just last week a patient told me that he never stops at red traffic signals unless there is other traffic in the opposite direction. He has received numerous traffic tickets but persists in this behavior. When I asked him why he did not obey the law like everyone else he replied, "But surely nobody stops at a red traffic signal if the intersection is clear. The law is an idiot, we should only obey it if it makes sense. It doesn't make sense to stop when there is no other traffic." I could not convince him that this was crooked thinking. For instance, how does he absolutely know that no other traffic is endangered? He only "thinks" that there is no oncoming traffic. His perceptions, like those of the rest of us, are not perfect. Only two months before, he had collided with another car when going through a red signal. He still can't believe that he missed seeing the oncoming car. The truth is that we all view the world from our own unique set of circumstances. We have our own beliefs about all sorts of things. This guarantees that we will all see things differently. Furthermore, we interpret what others say and do from the perspective of our own beliefs and wants. We actually distort what we see and hear to fit what we think is happening.

For example, if we are hungry, we are likely to interpret everything with food in mind. If we need love, we are likely to see it in the eyes or hear it in the voices of others. If we've been rejected in a relationship, we are likely to be very cautious about all other relationships.

In essence, what I am saying is that our picture of reality is shaped very much by our previous experiences. And since we all have had different and unique experiences, each of us will have a unique and highly individualistic point of view of reality. To each of us, therefore, reality will look different than it does to everyone else.

To think correctly means we must be able to understand the influence of past experiences on present beliefs and be able to sift through them and find an uncontaminated truth. It is these past experiences that cause us to make assumptions about the present, assumptions that can be erroneous and even dangerous.

Crooked thinkers also assume that others know everything they know. You hear them say, "But I thought you knew I meant we would meet at the restaurant on Baker Street." Or, "But you know I always do my banking on Tuesdays." Another favorite is "Didn't you know that John had asked me to have dinner with him after work? You were in the room when I talked with him on the phone. You must have heard our conversation. Therefore, you must have known what was happening . . ."

These thinkers expect you to be a mind reader. You are supposed to know, and they assume you know, everything.

Needless to say, many conflicts arise. If you are married to an assumptive thinker, you will have many hassles over these "but I thought you knew" assumptions. You will be late ("I thought you knew I would be there by 5"), you will buy the wrong size ("I thought you knew I took a size 16 shirt"), and you will invite the wrong guests ("I thought you knew I didn't like Billy anymore"). The words *I thought* are the major elements of the assumptive thinker's vocabulary.

Assumptive thinkers will also offend, hurt, and disrupt relationships. These qualities are not conducive to success of any sort. If you are such a person, the solution is to admit it and work at improving your basic communication skills. Do *not* assume that others know what you know. You need to work at telling people what it is you are assuming. Ask others to be direct in getting information from you. "Please tell me what time you will be home." "Please tell me where we will be meeting." Be specific in getting information. Be accurate in giving it. *Never* assume, when you can check it out. Ask, "Did I give you the key?" It doesn't matter if you have already asked but forgotten the answer. Redundancy is the best antidote for assumptive thinking. Very few people complain about having too much information!

Crooked Thinking Is Rigid Thinking

Crooked thinkers tend not to change their minds very often, and this lack of flexibility will work against them. I know that there is another side to this coin. One can be so flexible as to be wishy-washy and never able to stick to any idea or project. That's another problem equally as inhibiting to the achievement of success. But if I were to choose between the two extremes, I would say that excessive rigidity is by far the more damaging.

When two people are opposed to each other in ideas or actions, there is more at stake than just their different points of view. There is a "resistance" to each other.

Resistance is an important concept to understand when dealing with people. It is all around us. We first learn it in infancy when we resist discipline, rules, requests, and the demands of others. It starts out as a form of self-protection. If we didn't resist some demands, we would become so scattered we could not accomplish anything. Later in life the tendency to resist becomes a habit and a major source of rigidity.

Often, rigidity occurs quite apart from the facts of a given situation. The facts can be totally contradictory, yet this thinker will continue to hold to a point of view. A healthy, reality-based thinker is willing to change his or her mind as often as the facts demand. After all, truth *is* reality, so why would one not embrace it?

The truth may not all be known at one time. If further truth becomes known, the sensible person will change his belief to fit this truth. One must be willing to change one's belief as often as new truth becomes known. This is honesty and this is thinking realistically. Of course, you don't change your point of view just because someone says you must or because some slight doubt is introduced. The truth must be clear and obvious to warrant change.

An example of how this works occurred only last week in my own life. Our seminary is planning a new building complex to house the Graduate School of Psychology. As dean of the school it is my responsibility to say how large the building should be. I opted for a very large building, stating that we needed room for future growth. "But how will you pay for the extra heating, cooling, and maintenance costs?" I was asked. I fumbled for an answer and became quite irrational. I wanted a larger building than we could immediately afford, and I became unresponsive to the reality of the situation. Reality says, "You can't have what you can't pay for!" Quickly I realized I was being irrational and engaging in crooked thinking. I changed my mind. I altered my request to be more in keeping with what we can afford. To change your mind when you have taken a firm position is hard. But successful people develop the ability to do it. It's the only way you can survive.

How can you tell when you are being a rigid crooked thinker? Here are three signs:

1. You are not open to new information. "Don't tell me, I don't want to hear" is what you say. You also withhold information so as to keep the truth from others. You have to, because if you did give out the correct information you might be forced to change your point of view.

2. You "objection hop." You jump from giving one objection to another. As soon as your opponent gives a response to your objection, you come up with another. You line your objections up one after the other to be shot out in machine-gun style as the opportunity arises. This is a sign of rigidity. You are not taking time to listen to your opposition, so you may be setting yourself up for a failure. *Everyone* has *some* wisdom to contribute. Make sure you take the time to listen—even if you don't agree with them.

3. You react with too much emotion. If you get angry in discussions, then it is safe to assume you are irrationally opposing something. Your buttons are being pushed and you feel out of control. Why else would you get angry? You get angry because you are losing and not getting your way. This is dangerous because it means you have lost your objectivity. Seldom (I'm not saying never, but seldom) do we get angry because we really care about an issue. We get angry mainly because we feel hurt, violated, or we can't have our way. Anger should signal a loud "be cautious" response in us. Something is wrong. Something is threatening us. The anger alerts us to this threat. Back off, regain your composure. Ask for a postponement of the decision. Take time to reconsider your actions. In a nutshell: cool off! Anger seldom solves problems, it only creates more.

Thinking Clearly

If you recognize any of these crooked-thinking tendencies as your habitual style, then you should consider changing. Knowing what you're doing is half the battle. The other half is practicing new ways of thinking.

Thinking can be practiced as easily as tennis, golf, or writing. In fact, I believe that colleges could teach classes in how to think straight. We should all be required to take regular refresher courses. We might have a more peaceful world. Believe me, we would reduce the incidence of neurosis significantly, and the average Christian's spiritual life would show a dramatic improvement in quality. The fact is that how we think influences our emotions and, consequently, our spiritual well-being very greatly.

Cognitive psychotherapy has become the major form of treatment for emotional problems. It deals primarily with the simple and basic ways in which we think. It is the primary therapeutic modality I use in my practice, and I believe it lends itself very well to the integration of the Christian point of view. It is an approach that emphasizes the centrality of thinking in all human functioning. It stresses that how we "frame" or give meaning to an incident in life determines its impact on us. Every sensible person knows this. It is not a new idea since it has been around ever since creation. But it is only in recent years that psychology has given attention to it.

For those readers who would seriously like to change their thinking habits, I have designed a series of exercises that will be presented in the following chapters. The exercises are based on the principles of the cognitive approach. They are easy to use and free of any inherent values since they are simply "ways of thinking." As a Christian you may engage in these exercises without any fear that your mind is being manipulated. You are totally, and at all times, in full control.

PART THREE
Using Reality Thinking to Change Your Life

In this section of the book I will discuss the practical benefits of being a "realistic thinker." There are many areas of life in which we can be "holistically successful." Because of the limitations of space I will focus on just a few. In chapter 8 I will discuss how our general physical health is influenced by our mind. We will see how stress is the product of our thinking. Since our emotions are important to every part of our being, this will be the subject of chapter 9. In chapter 10 I will provide practical exercises for changing thinking patterns by showing how the "stream of our thought" can be influenced. Finally, in chapter 11 I will address the importance of finding and knowing God's purpose for your life. We will see how this can improve your self-esteem in an appropriate Christ-like way.

My purpose is clearly described in the Living Bible's translation of Romans 5, verse 2, where Paul says:

> For because of our faith, he has brought us into this place of highest privilege where we now stand, and we confidently and joyfully look forward to *actually* becoming *all* that God has had in mind for us to be (italics added).

I can think of no greater way of achieving success than this!

Controlling Stress Through Reality Thinking

Chapter 8

Modern science is moving us ever closer to the acceptance of an age-old truth: The body is the *servant* of the mind. Do you grasp this truth? The body obeys the operations of the mind. In many complex and wonderful ways, *what* we think and *how* we think is translated into health or sickness within every structure that makes up our human frame.

This is why we are discovering that stress can be so devastating. The way we approach life, perceive what is happening to us, and respond to its demands can wreak havoc in our cardiovascular, gastrointestinal, respiratory, and other systems. Our attitudes and general beliefs become transformed by a complex connection between the mind and the body into messengers that carry sickness or health to our tiniest cells.

Thoughts can disturb the balance of our bodies. They can rob us of necessary defenses against disease. They can divert healing mechanisms from critical life-supporting organs so that we succumb to infections. Literally, the mind has great control over the body.

I discovered this truth very personally two years ago while undergoing a routine physical examination. The doctor mentioned that my EKG showed a slight irregularity, in that my heart occasionally skipped a beat. He assured me it was a normal response. Many people had it and there was no pathological cause.

I went home, at first feeling contented. Then, as I lay down to sleep, I began to think. My self-conversation went as follows: "I suppose I'm OK ... if there were something wrong the doctor would have started treatment ... could he be withholding information ... how do I know he didn't call my wife to warn her I'm done for ... I'm sure I am a very sick person ..." and so on. Very soon my heart was racing and doing all sorts of funny things. This convinced me further that I was in serious trouble.

It was weeks before I finally got over my exaggerated reaction. My body began to panic because my mind was panicking. I think I could have thought my way into the grave, such was my mind's power.

The Body and the Mind

The body responds in a thousand ways to the stream of our thought. It is aroused or calmed, threatened or subdued, made anxious or tranquilized by the ideas that pass through our mind. Whether these thoughts are deliberately created or automatically and unconsciously experienced seems to make little difference. What we are discovering is that increased proneness to disease can be the final consequences of mental activity, just as much as it can be of bacteria or cell deterioration.

For centuries we have known that when people are subjected to unhealthy and negative thoughts, their bodies begin to respond with disease-producing mechanisms. When the thoughts are healthy, positive, creative, pure, and happy, the body moves toward youthfulness and health again. This awareness led James

Allen, a turn-of-the-century minister, to write in *As a Man Thinketh*, "If you would protect your body, guard your mind. If you would renew your body, beautify your mind." In many ways, he was anticipating the connection between the mind and the body, which only now we are beginning to fully appreciate. We have only just begun to unravel this marvelous but very complex interconnection. We need to be successful in achieving a harmony between the two.

The Errors of Christian Science

I need to make very clear, at this point, that I do not agree with the teachings of Christian Science. When I say that the mind can influence the disease- or health-producing mechanisms of our bodies, I do not mean to imply that we can stop the natural aging process or that sickness can be avoided.

Christian Science, also known as the Church of Christ, Scientist, adheres to a different, and to my mind, destructive set of beliefs. Its founder, Mary Baker Eddy, was born in a New Hampshire village in 1821. She was sickly as a child and later was given to frequent "nervous attacks." She married young and was tragically widowed at twenty-three. Nine years later she was married again, this time to a dentist. Gradually, she slipped into invalidism and isolation.

At the age of forty-one she met Phineas Quimby, a simple, self-educated handyman from Maine who repaired clocks while he dabbled in "mind cures." She claims that she was healed after being instructed by him and reading an account of a healing by Jesus. This transformed her life and she began to teach her strange beliefs about sickness and healing. After encouraging others to adopt her beliefs, she founded her church in Boston in 1882.

Many commentators believe that what Mary Baker Eddy experienced at the hands of Phineas Quimby was nothing more than was later to be called *psychotherapy*—hardly anything miraculous. Yet she believed differently, as did her many followers.

She developed a system of so-called "healing" based on her notion that all "matter" is mortal error. Anything that is physical and material is "unreal." It should be very clear to the reader that the teachings of Christian Science encourage the exact opposite of what I do. They foster a denial of reality. In Christian Science the mind is used to deny that disease or sickness exists. If you deny it, it is supposed to go away. This is quite the opposite of reality thinking, where the acceptance of the inevitability of sickness and disease is encouraged and where stress is minimized by being realistic. There is abundant evidence that admitting to reality and adopting an attitude of control over life's circumstances is less stress producing than avoidance.

The Mind and Disease

In no field of science has proof for a link between the mind and disease been more evident than in the fledgling field of *psychoneuroimmunology*. It's a long word, but we better learn it because we'll be hearing a lot more about it in the future. Here, psychologists and immunologists are collaborating in their research and making some very remarkable and mind-boggling discoveries.

The immunological system of the body is that system responsible for fighting disease. It is the body's protective mechanism comprising a highly complicated, finely tuned system of cells and chemistry that intercommunicate to keep us alive by fighting off illness.

In times past we believed that the mind was separate from the body. They were dual and independent. Disease was always thought of as purely physical. But doubts always lingered in human minds. Certainly, scripture never taught this. A refusal to accept any notion of dualism led primitive people to utilize the power of the mind. They discovered that magic spells could kill their enemies. Chicken soup could cure strange maladies. Rituals of all sorts could keep people from dying of real illnesses. The power to accomplish this was not in the spell, soup, or ritual, but in the fact that the victims or patients *believed* that what was to happen would in fact happen.

So we are now here: The mind can both cure and destroy. If healthy thoughts can heal, then troubled thoughts can disturb the healing resources of the body. Some have even gone so far as to suggest that the mind could destroy the body by turning it against itself. Such cases are known as *autoimmune* diseases.

Rediscovering the Mind's Power

Much experimental evidence now exists to show how the immune system is influenced by the mind. It is not my intention here to prove this point by citing this research to any extent. The interested reader can consult the many books now available on this topic. Let me just briefly mention a few fascinating discoveries so that I might convince you of the mind's ability to affect your body.

In animal research, mice have been taught how to suppress or enhance their own immune systems on command. Chickens subjected to the stress of a new pecking order have been shown to have a marked increase in the risk of disease. Bighorn sheep placed in captivity experience a reduction in their immune activity for at least two months afterward.

In humans, bereavement has been demonstrated to reduce resistance to illness. For example, the husbands of women who died from breast cancer showed marked reductions in white blood cell counts (part of the immune system) in the two months following the death of their spouse. The return to normal of their immune systems occurred only after the fourth month.

The idea that the emotions are related to the onset and course of cancer is also being researched. Many studies looking at the relationship of psychological factors (particularly stress) to the onset of cancer are now underway. What is the effect of the mind on the development of cancer? We don't know yet, but there is a strong possibility that a healthy mind can maximize the protection of the immune system to fight off cancer, even when the predisposition to the disease is genetically determined.

Good psychological health is the basis for good physical health! When coupled with good nutrition, healthy habits, and the avoidance of damaging stress, physical well-being can achieve its highest potential. The Christian life encourages precisely this. God knows how He has created us. His Gospel, through Christ, is designed in a wonderful way to encourage the very life-style that produces harmony between the mind and the body.

First Things First

James Allen wrote, "Change in diet will not help a man who will not change his thoughts." I believe this to be true.

A prominent and very successful Christian businessman came to see me recently. He had just turned fifty and was experiencing the throes of a mid-life crisis. A year before, he had decided to change his life-style. He realized his health was deteriorating, so he began exercising, changed his eating habits, and lost all his surplus fat. He cut back on his social engagements, quit his secret smoking habit, and reduced his working hours.

But this new life-style only helped a little. Sure, he felt physically better. He could run a mile. He could bound up his office stairs and not be embarrassed by being out of breath when he encountered his secretary. He could go to a restaurant and limit his food intake even though everyone else gulped greedily. But he still didn't "feel right." His heart skipped beats, he was tense and uptight, he experienced frequent headaches, and his temper flared at the slightest provocation. He disliked being with people.

What was wrong? Why didn't the changes he had made make any difference? Why was he still unhappy? Why did he feel he was still deteriorating physically? These questions bothered him greatly.

There are no simple answers. As we explored his attitudes and feelings, it appeared that he was harboring a lot of resentment.

He hated his mother. He detested his younger sister. He had grown to dislike his wife, and even his grown-up children irritated him. He was boiling with rage. Deep anger consumed him. He seldom recognized these feelings. In fact, he had hardly any awareness of them at all. He thought these were just normal feelings. He had bottled up his rage for so long it was now turning against him. His anger and hostility were backfiring, and he was in the line of the backfire. He had tried to create a healthy body, but his mind had been left to go its own way. Finally, it overcame his body. It proved to be the master.

As we talked about his feelings and how they were created by his thinking, he slowly began to resolve his anger and distorted view of life. Marvelously his body began to respond. His blood pressure lowered to normal. His sleeping habits improved. His priorities changed. Once again he was in touch with reality, and his physiology responded by restoring itself to a healthful state.

Was I surprised? Not really. In my work as a Christian psychologist I help many to achieve healthy bodies through healthy thoughts and a mature spirituality. It is not sufficient to take care of the body. You can jog, eat right, avoid alcohol, take vitamins and regular vacations, but none of these, nor all of them together, will help you completely unless you begin to change how you think.

Stress and Illness

Of all the many ways in which the mind can cause the body to become ill, the most common is through the way we handle stress. Prolonged stress will produce illness if it is not managed correctly, as surely as dark clouds rain.

A recent report in *Time* magazine (June 6, 1983) on the problem of stress stated that the three best-selling drugs of our nation today are Tagamet (an ulcer medication), Inderal (for lowering high blood pressure), and Valium (a minor tranquilizer). These three drugs help to treat the three major consequences of chronic stress, namely, excessive stomach acid that can cause ulcers, elevated blood pressure, and extreme agitation and anxiety. These problems are all stress related. They result from the prolonged triggering of the body's emergency system called the "fight or flight" response.

Whenever the mind senses a threatening event, it causes the body to release various hormones for the purpose of mobilizing its defenses. One of these is adrenaline, which increases the heart rate, raises the blood pressure, and releases sugar for energy. Most of us recognize this response as a flood of energy that propels us to action. We either perform some feat of strength or endurance, or we tackle an annoying person and get angry. Sometimes we just plain run away!

Now, after we have acted, the body calms down again and restores its normal, nonaroused condition. If we don't act, or our action is ineffective, or if there is nothing to act against, our body continues to maintain this fight-or-flight response, chemicals continue to be released, and this finally produces some breakdown of the body's organs. This is known as "distress" and it is produced by a chronic state of stress arousal. Unfortunately, our modern life-style produces a lot of it. We don't know how to escape from it, and we are too busy creating more of it through our hectic, rapid-paced busyness.

It is a sorry sign of modern times and the human condition, that our stress is out of control. Indeed, over the past thirty years medical science has come to realize just how heavy a toll stress is taking on our well-being. According to the American Academy of Family Physicians, two-thirds of office visits to family doctors are occasioned by stress-related symptoms. It is known to be a major contributor, either directly or indirectly, to six of the leading causes of death in the United States—coronary heart disease being number one.

Symptoms of Distress

Of the less serious, but still debilitating, consequences of stress the following would all be considered to have stress as a component in their cause or aggravation. Review this list and see whether you suffer from any of these symptoms:

- Headaches
- Migraines
- Ulcers
- Heartburn
- High blood pressure
- Chronic fatigue
- Jaw tension and teeth grinding (bruxism)
- Back and shoulder pains due to muscle tension
- Digestive disorders
- Constipation
- Diarrhea
- Frequent colds and bouts of influenza
- Panic anxiety

It is quite a formidable list! Almost by the month some new understanding of how stress contributes to these problems is added.

Basically, the physical problems following stress are caused by three important consequences of a prolonged fight-or-flight response. An understanding of these will help you manage your stress better.

1. Stress affects the body's ability to fight disease by depleting the immune system. This causes you to become prone to frequent illnesses like the flu and colds.

2. Stress depletes the brain's natural painkillers. Known as *endorphins,* these analgesics provide an important protection against pain. This causes you generally to experience more pain, including in the joints and muscles.

3. Stress depletes the brain's natural tranquilizers that help to keep us calm and peaceful. Not only does this cause us to become anxious and jittery, but it sets up further stress leading to further damage.

Should Christians Be Free of Stress?

Ideally, the answer is yes. In reality, Christians must live in a stress-producing world like everyone else, so they will be subject to many of the same pressures.

We should remember that it is not stress itself that is the killer, but our reaction to it. Some stress is essential to life. Without it we would fade away. Some stress is good for us. It stimulates the system and gives us energy. It is the consequence of prolonged stress not handled properly that does the damage.

Our walk with Christ provides many important resources to reduce the impact of life's pressures. Our value system should help to diminish the importance of material things. Our ability to love should make us tolerant of the mistakes of others. And our regular use of prayer and Christian meditation should help us to keep our perspective and restore an inner tranquility.

Many Christians feel guilty because they are stressed. They erroneously believe that they should be the master of every life problem, never experience anxiety or depression, and never be bothered by any irritation. This expectation is unrealistic and creates more stress. Some stress is inevitable in life and essential to survival. Living a godly life in a sinful and cruel world will have its share of problems. But if we are able to receive forgiveness for our waywardness, not demand too much perfection from our inadequate selves, and always keep God at the center of our lives, we can keep the damaging consequences of distress at a minimum.

Thoughts and Stress

There are many causes of stress, and since I cannot address them all here, my focus will be on how thoughts can cause stress and how they can be used to counteract distress.

Everything about us is taken in through the senses (sight, hearing, touch, smell, and so forth). When something happens to us, we always engage in some *thought* before it has any effect on us. Our thinking may appear to be very quick and cause an almost instant reaction, but it is thought nevertheless. This understanding is crucial to providing us with a solution to the problem. It means that by changing the way we think, especially the beliefs and attitudes that underly our thinking, we can interpose an effective "stress filter" that can remove threats or reduce the impact of an external event on our stress-response mechanisms.

For example, if I am driving on the freeway and some reckless driver suddenly turns in front of me, instead of my immediate fear reaction giving way to intense anger at the recklessness of his behavior, I can choose the attitude: "Some people are careless. I am only thankful that I escaped injury." I can create this attitude by believing that getting angry does not change reckless drivers into careful ones. Anger only causes me stress and makes me careless in turn. We will explore how to create a healthy attitude, in a short while.

Thoughts Can Be Stressors

Not only do thoughts turn external events into stressors, but thoughts themselves can cause stress. Our bodies will react to the threat of what we think as readily as to the threat of what we see.

What are some of the more common thoughts that consistently cause stress? I have categorized them into three groups.

1. *Aiming too high.* Unrealistic goals can set us up to experience frequent frustrations and disappointments. If we expect too much from ourselves or others, we will frequently experience the stress of disappointment.

As humans we are very hard on ourselves. Perhaps it is because our parents demanded too much from us, just as their parents demanded too much from them. Perhaps it's because we all want to be gods—perfect, capable, competent, and worshiped by everybody. Whatever the reason, to keep our stress low we should learn to be realistic about our abilities. Exaggerated ambition is very often a compensation for low self-esteem. We want to prove to the world that we are somebody. We want to establish our immortality by making our mark on history. Our thoughts become preoccupied with accomplishing some great goal.

Unfortunately, most of us are doomed to never achieving perpetual recognition. Is this bad? Not if we have our priorities straight. Not if we accept that the solution to our low self-esteem does not lie in achieving some great honor, but in totally accepting who we are in God's sight.

2. *Condemning too hard.* We are a critical and judgmental people. We want everything to be perfect, and if it isn't we complain bitterly. We condemn others when they do not live up to our expectations. This makes us irritable and angry. It arouses our fight-or-flight mechanisms even further. Not only does the original aggravation cause us stress, but our need to attack the cause of the aggravation compounds it further.

We are, perhaps, hardest on ourselves. Most of us have a deep need to condemn ourselves whenever we fail. We engage in self-punishment for not meeting the standards (many of them ridiculous) we have set for ourselves. While this may be an internalizing of early parental treatment, I sometimes think it is a part of our lower nature wanting to play God.

Whatever the cause, the solution is the same: *forgiveness.* To be an unstressed, healthy person, you need to know how to forgive and receive forgiveness—from God, others, and yourself. Forgiveness limits our stress. It contains it, so that it does not go further than it should. It also helps to restore our body's balance because it takes away the need for revenge and robs resentment of its power to destroy us.

It was Hans Selye, the "father" of stress research, who said that among all the emotions, the one that most accounts for the presence of harmful stress is the feeling of hatred and the urge for revenge. Hans, you're a little late. God has been telling us that since creation—the trouble is we won't hear it!

3. *Fearing the unlikely.* Thoughts about the future can also cause stress. They cause us to fight unnecessary battles and flee from imaginary foes, not once but many times. Nothing is more stressful to the body than imagined fear and anxiety. It triggers the adrenal system and then prolongs the adrenaline's presence in the body because the imagined crisis never comes to an end. This prolonged adrenal arousal is known to do the following:

- Encourages blood clotting, thus increasing the risk of heart attacks and strokes
- Narrows blood vessels, so that the blood cannot nourish some parts of the body
- Releases fatty deposits that narrow the arteries
- Raises blood pressure that can cause damage to the brain and kidneys

This is why "worry thinkers" are living dangerously. They might as well go and play on the freeway; they are running the same risk of damaging themselves!

The solution? Learn how to be less anxious. In the final analysis, good stress management is as much a matter of faith as it is of learning how to rest and relax. If you don't believe in God, then it's going to be very hard. What else is there to give you hope? For the Christian, provision has been made for us to minimize our unnecessary fears about unlikely future happenings.

"In nothing be anxious," says Paul, "but in every thing by prayer and supplication with thanksgiving let your requests be made known unto God" (Philippians 4:6).

Those who really know how to do this are least troubled by stress.

Distress Is in the Little Things

The notion that major life events are the cause of stress illness is widespread yet grossly misleading, if not wrong. Recent research has shown that it's the day-to-day hassles—having a fight with your kids, getting stuck in traffic, missing the bus, losing your keys, dropping a camera, running out of gas, getting a flat tire, and letting your coffee get cold—that can kill you.

Yes, this is true! Everyday tensions, and how we react to them, make us the stress-prone people we are. How can you know if these hassles get to you? Here is a brief test I have devised. See how you score:

Everyday-Hassles Test

	YES	NO
1. Are you friendly toward *all* your neighbors and work colleagues?	☐	☐
2. Do you, on a daily basis, enjoy your work?	☐	☐
3. Do you feel financially secure?	☐	☐
4. Does life seem meaningful most of the time?	☐	☐
5. Do you feel in control of your life?	☐	☐
6. Must you combine housekeeping or parenting with having to earn a living?	☐	☐
7. Are you a single parent?	☐	☐
8. Do you feel angry toward someone or irritated by something at least once a day?	☐	☐
9. Do you often have sleepless nights? More than once a week?	☐	☐
10. Are you always in a hurry?	☐	☐

Give yourself one point for each "no" answer on questions 1 to 5 and "yes" answers on questions 6 to 10.

If you score 7 to 10 points, you are the victim of a lot of stress. Beware: you need to change radically. If your score is 5 to 6, your stress levels are moderate and you need to change some aspect of your life. If you are below 4, you are average, but the lower the better. If you score zero, the chances are that you are either hibernating or else you have developed a remarkably calm and placid personality.

Managing Stress Through Reality Thinking

One cannot avoid stress altogether, but we can control our re-action to it. At the heart of all good stress management are the following: learning how to relax, reducing weight, eating healthy food, exercising, reducing work hours, and changing *how* you think. It's this last step we are interested in here.

Many of the exercises I will describe in later chapters will sig-nificantly reduce your stress level, since a calm mind creates a stress-free body. Here are some further suggestions:

1. *Reality Testing.* When confronted by an obstacle, con-flict, or hassle, the first step is to ask yourself:

"What is reality here?" As I have emphasized throughout this book, God has designed us to deal with reality, not imagination. Reality has solutions. There are no answers or solutions to fan-tasy. If you know what reality is, the solution is often an obvious next step. It may not be a pain-free solution, but in the long run you will feel more in control.

Don't avoid reality. Don't fall into the trap of thinking that just because many people say something is a certain way, that it is so. Consensus doesn't create reality. Life is manageable, liv-able, stress free and most times extremely satisfying if we learn to live with reality.

2. *Modify Your Values.* Our values control us. They deter-mine our expectations and our priorities.

Some years ago I served on the board of a professional organi-zation with another psychologist. We became good friends. He was extremely ambitious and hardworking. He never stopped, seldom took a vacation, and his seven-days-a-week regimen of committees, patients, lecturing, and writing satisfied him deeply.

"Peter," I asked him once, "why do you do it? Are you sure that the rewards are worth it?"

He smiled and nodded his head, and I never really knew what he meant.

I began to feel guilty. How come I never worked this hard? Sundays I went to church. Should I rather see needy patients and serve God rather than worship Him?

Then one day I got the answer. Peter, still a young man, had a massive heart attack. For six months he could not work and I never saw him at board meetings. When finally he emerged from his convalescence, he was a changed man. He was extremely thin, of course, but I mean he had changed his values. He had decided to work only thirty hours a week and modify his standard of living to match his reduced income. He moved slowly, took his time over lunch, and never seemed irritated.

When I asked him how this change had come about, he replied, "You cannot stand at the brink of your own death and not be affected by it." His values were never the same again.

Must we be brought face-to-face with eternity before we realize how our values can destroy us? Take a moment to reflect on what you want out of life. Make a list of your priorities. Make a long list! Then prayerfully consider each item. Decide—is this really necessary? If it isn't, cut it out of your life. If it is, then go for it—prayerfully and in deep commitment to God.

3. *Filter Your Stressors.* Our mind can be a big stress filter. Since everything must pass through it, it can screen out unwanted material if we so teach it. When something bothers us, we can ask, "Is it necessary to get upset?" When something irritates us, we can say, "Is getting angry going to solve anything?" When we feel out of control, we can remind ourselves, "Who is really in control? Need I panic when I know my Lord is with me?"

Positive and healing self-talk is therefore a great stress antidote. So is changing your attitudes.

I used to get very angry driving on the freeway during rush hours. Crowding bothered me and inconsiderate drivers drove me up the wall. I realized my stress was killing me, not them, so I modified my work schedule so that I traveled to and from work when the freeway wasn't crowded.

That was one solution. Then I realized that a better way would be to change my attitude toward the crowded freeway. Coming home late at night was hardly a good solution! I decided I would enjoy the crowded road. I would take some tapes for listening and use the time for prayer and meditation. Now I listen to lectures on theology, sermons my friends have preached, lectures my students give at churches, and music, while slowly making my way home in the slow lane. I love this time and am even disappointed when it is over. What was stressful has become a blessing—all because I changed my attitude.

We can do this for many life situations—an unhappy marriage, problem children, a miserable work situation, or an incurable illness. If you can't change your circumstances, change your attitude toward them.

Stress Can Be Your Ally

Space does not permit me to provide further discussion of the many ways we can reduce the harmful consequences of stress. This will have to be another book project. Let me close by helping you understand that stress is your ally and that you learn from it.

Stress, and the response of your body, is really your friend. Heed the signals of your body. Headaches are telling you something. Ulcers are demanding attention. High blood pressure beckons you to change your life-style and thinking.

Overcoming stress is a slow process of mental change in which you focus on calming techniques, learn to walk and talk more slowly, improve your listening and communication skills, and force yourself to relax periodically. The same Jesus who said, "Go ye into all the world and preach the gospel" (see Mark 16:15), also said, "Come ye apart and rest awhile" (see Mark 6:31). Why do we so easily forget this?

We must also learn to organize our time better, set clearer priorities, and talk nicely to ourselves. Remember, if you enjoy what you are doing, stress can be good for you. If you don't, it can kill you.

John, the apostle, tells us, "Count it all joy, my brethren, when you meet various trials . . ." (James 1:2 RSV).

Perhaps he knew that damaging stress could not coexist with joy.

How the Stream of Thought Affects Your Emotions

Chapter 9

In recent years there has been a dramatic change in the way psychologists view emotion. We have rediscovered that normal emotions are the end product of what we think. Imagine that! You feel what you think! And all the time Scripture has told us this. "For as he thinketh in his heart, so is he," said Solomon, the son of David, king of Israel, more than three thousand years ago (Proverbs 23:7).

Even so, this rediscovery is still liberating, because ever since the early days of Sigmund Freud, we have been told that our emotions are dark secrets created by unconscious and mysterious forces over which we have no control. Even worse, our emotions are so obscure and hidden from us that we don't even know what we are feeling. Frightening, isn't it? Only if you believe it!

But this is changing. No longer do we believe that our emotions are victimized by concealed forces beyond our awareness. Our emotions are not mysterious and intricate but straightforward and easy to understand. They are the natural consequences of very natural processes. Furthermore, the normal range of emotions that we all experience, *can* be controlled. This control is possible because we can control our thinking. The implications of this for holistic success are enormous.

Which Emotions Cannot Be Controlled?

It is not possible to control all emotions, nor should we try to. Many painful emotions are quite beyond voluntary control. Some are caused by biological factors. If, for example, I am feeling depressed at the same time that I have the flu, I probably am experiencing an emotion that is a symptom of an underlying illness. To cure the emotion I have to cure the underlying illness. It is normal that we should experience these emotions. They are protective signals that must be heeded.

Furthermore, our feelings are not simply "in our heads." They are the consequence of many complicated electrical, biochemical, and other changes in many parts of our body. Parts of the brain, the endocrine system, and even the state of tension in our muscles all contribute to our emotional experience. Together they determine what we feel.

While these biological states can be created by what we think, and mostly they are, it is possible for a part of our body to be diseased or dysfunctional and for this, and only this, to be the cause of our emotional state. The healthiest thing we can do with these states is to accept them.

Our "normal" feelings are a different story! These are the result of what goes on in our thinking, and we literally create or eradicate them a thousand times every day, without even knowing what is going on in our thoughts.

Where Is Your Treasure?

Marcus Aurelius (A.D. 121–180), one of the more humane of the Roman emperors, wrote in his *Meditations*, "If you are pained by an external thing, it is not the thing that disturbs you—but your judgment about it." By *judgment,* of course, he means how you *think* about, and the value you place upon, the external thing. To change how you think about the event is to change how you feel.

Emotions are the consequence of the meanings (or beliefs) we attach to events, not the events themselves. I believe that this idea is thoroughly biblical. The Gospel places great emphasis on the importance of the meaning we attach to things, because this determines how we feel about them. In the sermon on the mount, Jesus reminds us of this when He says, "Lay not up for yourselves treasures upon earth ... But lay up for yourselves treasures in heaven.... For where your treasure is, there will your heart be also" (Matthew 6:19–21). Remember, Scripture often equates the heart with the mind. In effect, Jesus is telling us that what we value will determine who we are, how we think, what gets our attention, and how we feel. These verses are then followed, in the same chapter, by a series of commands about how we should think:

"Take no thought for your life ..." (verse 25).

"Which of you by taking thought ..." (verse 27).

"And why take ye thought for raiment ..." (verse 28).

"Therefore take no thought ..." (verse 31).

"Take therefore no thought for the morrow ..." (verse 34).

These are all commands against the type of thinking we call worrying but can better be translated "anxious thought." Of the painful emotions we are all prone to, anxious worrying must surely be the most common. Clearly, this anxiety is fed by the way we think. We have learned how to think in a worrying way.

Reality thinking is a way out of this pain. To think realistically may be fear provoking, but fear is easier to deal with than anxiety. Fear is tangible, anxiety is vague and intangible. Successful people cannot afford to spend too much time in "worry pain." It saps energy and takes attention away from more important things.

Thoughts and Emotions

It is very easy to demonstrate to yourself how feelings can be created by thinking. Go for a walk and recall some meaningful early-childhood experiences. Think about it for a while. Try to recall all the details. Then stop and note what you are feeling. What were you feeling when you started your walk? What are you feeling now? The change will be due to your thinking.

Or, think of an old friend (better not make it a current one) and begin to recall all the negative things about him or her you can remember. Think about them for a while. Very soon you will start feeling all sorts of negative emotions—anger, hate, or disgust—depending on the history of experiences you have had with your friend. These will be due entirely to your thinking.

Now, stop thinking about the negative experiences and start to recall all the positive things you can remember about your friend. Continue to think about them for a while. Soon your feelings will become positive. You are likely to feel warm, loving, and friendly toward your friend.

Try this exercise a few times until you are convinced that you can create or remove your feelings by what you think.

Feelings Follow Beliefs

The cognitive approach to psychotherapy emphasizes that every emotional reaction is the inevitable consequence of our beliefs and attitudes. They are not the consequence of a particular action or event.

For instance, if a friend tells you she hates you, you are likely to become very upset. You will feel miserable. But! It will not be the words of your friend that will cause you to feel this way. The message may be the *trigger* for what follows, but your consequent feeling will actually be created by what you believe and how you think about the message. It is because you expect to be liked by your friend that the rejection bothers you. If the same message came from someone you knew to be an enemy, your expectation would be different—and so would your feeling.

This is where psychological actions are different from physical actions. In the physical realm, if you slap me I will hurt. The slap is the direct cause of my hurt. In the psychological realm, words are only symbols—they do not hurt directly. Verbal slaps must have meaning attached to them or else they don't hurt. It is this "meaning" we attach to words, out of our beliefs, attitudes, expectations, and assumptions, that gives them the power to create emotions in us.

This is both good news and bad news. The bad news is that psychological hurt is not as easy to avoid as physical hurt. You can always run away from someone who wants to hit you! The good news is that since psychological hurt is mainly caused by words, we *can* easily learn how to minimize or avoid hurt altogether. It is just a matter of attaching new meanings to the old words that bother us.

This is what reality thinking is all about. Since the meanings we attach to words and ideas are often irrational and unrealistic, it is little wonder that we experience as much emotional turmoil as we do. Attention to a few basic rules can significantly change these meanings. With the Holy Spirit to help us in this, we can revolutionize our minds, create healthy attitudes, and thus live more meaningful and happy lives.

The Stream of Thought

Imagine that the activity of your mind is like a stream that flows past your consciousness. Psychologists call this the *stream of thought,* because it is exactly this. It starts somewhere out of consciousness, passes the window of your awareness, and then moves on again out of your consciousness to influence some other part of your being.

Sometimes it is a small stream. Your mind is quiet and there is little activity. Consequently your whole being is peaceful and nonaroused. At other times it can become a raging torrent.

Thoughts flood your head to the point that you feel it will burst. The thoughts may even be turbulent and fast flowing. They tumble over each other, eroding everything in their way, and making you feel very unsettled. It seems that even in sleep this stream continues to flow, feeding dreams and other thought activity.

The key to controlling your emotions, and literally making you who you want to be, lies in learning how to control this stream of thought.

You Never Stop Thinking

You are always thinking. It is a continuous stream. The source of the stream of thought is a mystery. To some extent you can voluntarily originate a thought. Consciously and deliberately, you can begin an idea and feed it into the stream. It can be any thought you choose. But there is much of the stream you can't control. It is involuntary. It starts by itself, deep within the mind, and continues whether you like it or not.

For instance, as I sit here writing I have suddenly experienced a flood of thoughts about my mother. She's been dead for ten years, and I doubt whether I have consciously thought about her much in the past year. Yet here are thoughts about her! I never chose them, they came by themselves. They flow strong. Memories come surging back to me, starting yet a chain of other thoughts.

Some of these thoughts bring pleasure. A few bring pain. I can do very little to control the origin of them. The fountain is way out of my reach. The point at which I do have control is where the stream passes my awareness. At this point I can reach in and remove what I don't want. I do not need to dwell on what I am thinking. I can set aside certain thoughts and even ignore them. The fountain will then begin to dry up.

Where Do Thoughts Go?

The destination of many thoughts is the body. In a mysterious way they become translated into body changes that can cause a reaction in every part of our being.

Thoughts also cause other reactions: fear, anxiety, depression, agitation, irritability, and anger, to name a few. Thoughts are not harmless. They influence every part of our being. A sour face is not a thing of chance. It is a reflection of sour thoughts.

To protect our emotions and our bodies we must guard our minds. We must encourage right thinking by feeding the stream of our thought with right thoughts. We must discourage wrongful thoughts by changing the beliefs and attitudes that give rise to them.

Paul, in his second epistle to the Corinthians, outlines the plan of action very clearly when he says:

". . . and bringing into captivity every thought to the obedience of Christ" (2 Corinthians 10:5).

The New English Bible translates it this way, ". . . we compel every human thought to surrender in obedience to Christ. . . ."

Notice *who* does the compelling. While we will need help from God in this, let us not minimize our role. God can only do in us what we allow Him to do. We are not puppets but freewill beings. We must begin by having an earnest desire on our part to change our thoughts.

Thoughts Create Thoughts

Thoughts can also become tributaries. This is the reverse of the natural river where tributaries usually feed into and become rivers.

In our thought life, rivers become tributaries in that thoughts lead to other thoughts. They "chain" from one idea to the next.

I mentioned a short while ago that as I was writing, I was flooded with thoughts about my mother—thoughts that also brought back many feelings. Well, these thoughts have since triggered other thoughts. Some about my father, brothers, grand-parents, early childhood, first day at school, and so on. Thoughts lead to thoughts. I used to have a patient who would often come into my office and say, "I've been *thinking* again!" By this she means that she has spent many hours dwelling on her thoughts. This inevitably makes her miserable. Whenever she thinks too much, she starts a chain of ideas that eventually causes her pain.

My strategy in therapy was to teach her how to distract her mind whenever she started on one of these thinking bouts. I taught her some of the exercises I will shortly describe, and she quickly learned to control this tendency.

Changing the Stream of Thought

Our thoughts have two main tributaries or sources. Examine the diagram below:

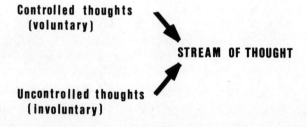

The first source is that of our *controlled thoughts*. These are thoughts that can be voluntarily generated. You have control over them since you can choose and deliberately encourage them any time you want. The truth is that you can begin to think about anything you choose at any time you want!

For instance, if I choose, I can begin to think about a happy childhood event. Let's say I want to think about the first time I ever went to the beach. I can recall it clearly. I was four or five years old. My parents gave me a small brightly colored tin bucket and a wooden spade (they use plastic buckets and spades these days—yuk!). I remember filling my bucket with wet sand and being shown how to turn it over and deposit a neatly shaped cone of sand on the beach. I repeated this many times all over until it seemed as though the whole beach was covered with my sand castles. What am I feeling? Very happy! I love this memory.

I deliberately chose to think about this event. It brings back pleasant feelings. But I can also stop at any point and start another thought. If this is true of pleasant thoughts, it is also true of unpleasant ones. Sounds simple? Yes, but this truth is so liberating that it needs to be sounded again and again.

The importance of all of this is that we can willfully begin to change the stream of our thought at any time we choose. We simply have to begin thinking about a pleasant or happy event. We have the power to originate this. Most unhappy people neglect to do it.

Uncontrolled Thoughts

The second source of the stream of thought is that of our *uncontrolled thoughts.* These thoughts are involuntary. They are not chosen or necessarily welcomed. Sometimes they intrude into your awareness like an unwanted burglar coming to rob you of your peace of mind. Sometimes they stay hidden, waiting until they can have their most damaging effect. Then they insidiously intrude.

A healthy mind can reduce the influence of these uncontrolled thoughts by ensuring that they are always "out in the open." By deliberately keeping them in our conscious awareness, they are easier to control and do not have the same damaging effect.

Exercises in Thought Control

You are now ready for exercises in learning how to change the stream of your thought. These exercises are based on the ideas I have presented thus far. They will increase your control over both the voluntary and involuntary source of your thinking. Work through them carefully as they are foundational for the exercises I will present in the next chapter.

EXERCISE 1

Purpose: To help you learn how to initiate pleasant thoughts whenever you choose. Initiating pleasant thoughts can help to displace unpleasant ones.

- *Step 1:* Take a card and write down five or six events you know will give you pleasure. These can be events from your past (memories of happy childhood outings) or present (your last visit to the beach or to a friend) or they may be events you anticipate with pleasure in your near future (such as an upcoming vacation).
- *Step 2:* Next to each pleasant event, write down two or three specific ideas or aspects of the event that interest or captivate you. For instance, if you are planning a vacation, you may wish to write down "plan clothes to be taken" or "examine travel brochure for places to visit" as specific ideas.
- *Step 3:* Keep this card with you at all times. Every hour or two, take out your card, select a pleasant event, and deliberately begin to think about one of the specific ideas you have written down. Take a moment to enjoy the feelings that it generates. Savor the pleasant feelings that follow. Try to think about it for four or five minutes. Then return the card to its place of safekeeping and go about your business.

Variations: Instead of places or events, make a list of personal qualities you would like to encourage in yourself. Would you like to be more loving? More caring? Ponder these. Or you may prefer to keep a favorite poem or portion of Scripture with you. Review these. Think about them deliberately and consciously.

EXERCISE 2

Purpose: Since involuntary thoughts are usually anxiety producing and create more anxiety if they are kept out of your awareness, this exercise will help you to bring them out "into the open."

• *Step 1:* Set aside twenty minutes for contemplation at the beginning and end of each day. Get yourself a small notebook specifically for this exercise, and during these periods of contemplation, write down *every* worry, anxiety, concern, bothersome thought, event, or person that comes into your mind. Your notebook will be confidential, so write down everything, no matter how petty it seems. Try to survey your day and recapture every troublesome thought.

• *Step 2:* Review your list of bothersome ideas. Ask yourself, "Which of these can I take care of right now? Is there anything I can change?" Then take that action immediately and cross that concern off your list.

• *Step 3:* Take a moment to pray about the rest of your list—those concerns you cannot take care of there and then. Commit to God any concern you cannot change. Then close your notebook and go about your business, trusting that God is in control of all you cannot control.

• *Step 4:* If any concern continues to bother you, make a note of it once more in your notebook. Then go to exercise 1, select a pleasant thought, and try to focus on that for a while.

Variation: I cannot stress strongly enough the value of writing down, as fully as possible, all thoughts and ideas that bother you. Writing them down helps to get them out of your memory where they will otherwise be kept alive by the memory-refreshing mechanisms of your brain. Your notebook, therefore, serves as an external memory. It can be taken with you everywhere.

A variation of this exercise is to use your notebook whenever you are bothered by a thought. As soon as it comes into your mind, write it down. It doesn't matter how often you write down the same thought—just keep doing it. This helps the brain to "give up" unwanted material as it knows that the information is being stored somewhere else.

Self-Talk

Before we proceed with further exercises, I need to explain one more very important thought mechanism. It is called *self-talk,* or *self-conversation.*

Many psychologists, especially those who use cognitive methods, emphasize that much of our thinking takes place in the form of a conversation with ourselves. We literally talk to ourselves all the time. This self-talk generates ideas that ultimately become translated into emotions. Since our reasoning is carried on as a conversation, you would think we could be aware of the content of the conversations. Unfortunately, unless we attend to our self-talk, we are not.

Furthermore, this self-talk is usually more irrational and illogical than conversations with others. We think more clearly when we talk to someone else than when we talk to ourselves. Often, when we share our feelings and thinking with someone else, we "see the light" and have a better understanding of what is happening to us. Suddenly, everything makes sense and we realize how ridiculous our reasoning has been.

We can become more aware of our thinking by learning how to attend to our self-conversations. We can then counter any disturbing self-talk in a rational and logical manner.

Let us suppose you have just had a conversation with a friend. Your friend has told you that she does not want to go to dinner with you next week. She is sorry she has had to cancel this engagement but something has come up. As you go back to your office desk, you begin to converse with yourself. The conversation may go something like this:

> I wonder why she doesn't want to go to dinner with me? She knows I planned this weeks ago. She knows how much I have looked forward to it. I wonder if her mother has been talking to her? I know she doesn't like me. What could her mother have said? Perhaps I didn't show enough enthusiasm over her garden—but would she hold this against me? Maybe I shouldn't have called so late the other evening.

Nothing ever goes right for me. Ever since I can remember, things have gone wrong. Life is terrible to me. I must be jinxed or something . . .

Very soon you are deeply depressed, although none of your thoughts are true.

Explore Your Self-Talk

Does the previous self-conversation sound ridiculous? Why don't you try writing down every conversation you have with yourself over your spouse, kids, boss, employees, pastor, or friends. You might be surprised at the sorts of things you say to yourself. It isn't until we see it written out that the irrationality becomes obvious. Think about the following characteristics of self-talk:

• Self-talk tends to be emotionally charged. It comes from hurts (real or supposed) and is fed by other feelings.

• Self-talk is fed by a vivid imagination. It seldom keeps in touch with reality. It exaggerates and oversensitizes us.

• Self-talk overgeneralizes. It takes one little event and tries to prove that everything is the same.

• Self-talk is irrational and illogical most of the time. It feeds off doubts and uncertainties and is seldom satisfied with reality.

• Self-talk usually leads to a "catastrophizing" of everything. It always ends, as my fictitious example does, with statements like "I am jinxed," or "I am terrible," or "Nobody cares for me."

• Self-talk is usually self-pitying and selfish. You are the center of the conversation and the focus of all offense, and you want to wallow in your mire and lick your wounds.

Improving Your Self-Talk

Healthy and successful people can recognize and stop their negative self-talk. They can analyze its content and argument, set aside the ridiculous and imagined, test reality and take whatever action needs to be taken, or inject healthier and more realistic ideas into the self-conversation. This keeps them from being influenced by evil thoughts.

Here is an exercise to help you monitor your self-talk.

EXERCISE 3

Purpose: To help you become aware of the conversations you have with yourself, especially those that are illogical and irrational.

• *Step 1:* Set an alarm or use some device to signal you at least once every hour. You can use class breaks, coffee breaks, or any other natural break in your day to signal the time for the exercise.

• *Step 2:* At the moment you are signaled, stop what you are doing and review very carefully the conversation you have been having with yourself during the previous five minutes. Write it down as sentences. Try to recall as many ideas or self-statements as possible. Pay particular attention to the conversation you are having with yourself at the moment the signal occurs.

• *Step 3:* Take your list of self-talk sentences and review each one. Ask yourself the following questions about them:

- Is it true?
- How do I know it is true?
- Is it reality?
- Am I overreacting?
- Will it be different tomorrow?
- Am I being sensible and realistic?
- What's the real issue?
- Where will this idea take me?

• *Step 4:* Deliberately counter your negative self-talk with positive, realistic, reassuring sentences. For example, say to yourself, "It is unfortunate that this has happened to me, but it is not the end." Or, "Who says I must be this way? I am being irrational and illogical and therefore I will not pay attention to what I am thinking."

A list of irrational self-statements is given at the end of chapter 10.

• *Step 5:* Find someone (a friend or spouse) to share your thoughts with. Irrational self-talk is best challenged in open conversation with another person. If no one is immediately available, share it with God. After all, this is what prayer is for.

Variation: You can monitor your self-talk at any time. Once you know how to do it when cued by set times, try catching your self-conversations at random times during the day. Monitor your self-talk while you are having a conversation with a friend or while standing in line at the supermarket. Generally, increase your awareness of what you say to yourself. This will help you to catch the stream of your thought.

Changing Old Habits

While the exercises I have described are fairly straightforward, some may find them difficult to perform. Old habits die hard. Many years of irrational self-talk are difficult to eradicate.

But don't lose heart if you don't change quickly! Nothing worthwhile is achieved without cost, so be patient and persistent. Master one step at a time.

Pray about your self-talk. God *is* interested in how you think and wants to renew your mind. You are not alone, therefore, in your endeavors.

In my next chapter I will continue to explore ways in which we can change our thinking. There will be more exercises to help you in this.

You Can Change Your Thoughts

Chapter 10

In the previous chapter I described how the stream of our thought is formed. I will now examine the ways in which our thoughts can be changed.

Our life in Christ is not just a set of moral standards which we must live up to. It is a spiritual reality, a TOTAL way of being. Christ will help us change our thinking as much as He will help us deal with sin. God, in Christ and by the action of His Holy Spirit, can perfect our being. He is the light that shows us the way and the strength that gives us the resource to change. He creates in us the desire to be like Him and then empowers us to attain this likeness. What a perfect gospel! There is none other like it.

As you examine your thought life and take steps to change it, do so with complete dependence on God to give you victory over your years of deeply ingrained habits. He longs to give you a renewing of your mind. *This* is reality! He wants to bring forth all the hidden and suppressed resources of your being. He wants to elevate and transfigure all the natural talents within you, glorifying them with the gifts of His grace.

I really do mean it when I say that *all* God needs is your coop-
eration, and you can discover and actualize your deep, real self.
Then surrender this self to His grace and discover that it multi-
plies like the loaves and fishes. You will find that there is more to
your existence than you ever dreamed possible. *This* is holistic
success!

Reviewing Reality

Before we start our exercises in reality thinking, let me make a
few general statements about my concept of *reality*.

For many, reality is a dirty word. It seems to mean the same as
"pessimistic" or "hopeless." It brings them down off their cloud
of possibility into the mud and mire of real life—or at least this is
what they think.

They are afraid of reality. It seems stark and scary, and quite
antiseptic. It might appear to rob life of fun and pleasure and
take away all enthusiasm and dreams. This is NOT what I mean
by reality.

Reality is simply truth. It is "things as they truly are." Reality
is honesty, openness, and frankness. It is hopeful where hope is
called for, faithful where faith is needed, and optimistic most of
the time. It is not a killjoy.

Reality is always fundamental to mental health. A popular
myth is that mental illness occurs when one is "too rooted in reality." That is, a person is bogged down by too much preoccupation with how life really is: stark and naked misery. This reality,
it is believed, creates fear and builds a prison of mental illness
around the person. The essence of normality, therefore, is the
"refusal of reality." This is just not true. The reality referred to
here is not reality at all. It is a grotesque exaggeration of all the
negative aspects of life. The Christian does not have to live at this
level. We don't have to become neurotic in order to transcend the
reality of our creatureliness. We have a life in Christ that tran-
scends our mortality. This is a different reality and it gives
meaning to all of life—including death.

You are not living in reality if you are too constricted to be who God wants you to be or if you have no forward momentum in your life. You cannot make free choices and grow where you need to grow. You are imprisoned by unreality. You are holistically unsuccessful. To think realistically is to unlock the prison gate and set yourself free. And if this freedom is coupled with the freedom Christ gives—then it is freedom indeed!

Exercises in Reality Thinking

There are five basic steps to be followed in taking control of the stream of your thought. These are:

1. Thought capturing

2. Thought evaluation

3. Thought challenging

4. Thought changing

5. Thought prevention

Combined, these exercises take you through a series of steps in which you capture a thought, evaluate it, challenge it if it isn't realistic, change it if necessary, and then prevent it from coming again. Learn each step first, before trying to combine them into a sequence of steps.

Let us go through each of the basic steps of taking control of your thinking.

1. THOUGHT CAPTURING

All thought control requires that we first be able to "capture" the stream of our thought. We must know *what* we are thinking before we can decide whether we want to change it or not.

The exercises presented in the previous chapter are exercises in thought capturing. They are designed to help you sample your thoughts at regular intervals. Review these exercises again and make sure you know how to implement them. You should be able, at will, to capture what you are thinking so that you can write it down without any trouble.

I will now suggest two further exercises that will help you accomplish this. The first is the use of an emotion as the starting point to the discovery of the thoughts leading up to it. The second is the use of bothersome, ruminating thought to discover the series of thoughts that preceded it. For both these exercises you will need pen and paper—so get that now. I will call this your thought notebook. Carry it with you at all times.

EXERCISE 4

Purpose: To discover the thought or thoughts that precipitated a particular emotional reaction.

- *Step 1:* When you realize you are having an emotional reaction, stop for a moment and label the emotion. This forces you to admit that you are feeling something. Write it down, whatever it is: "I am angry"; "I am depressed"; "I feel guilty"; "I feel lonely"; or "I feel hatred." This step is important because we tend as Christians not to want to admit to ourselves that we are feeling a negative emotion. Of course, you can also write down positive emotions and help to build your awareness of these.
- *Step 2:* Ask yourself: "Why am I feeling this way?" All emotions, particularly the negative ones, are *signals*. They are telling you that something is wrong and action is needed. Write down as many reasons as you can think of.
- *Step 3:* Now ask yourself: "What thoughts led up to my present feeling?" Try to identify the chain of ideas that preceded the emotion. Perhaps someone criticized your work or idea. What did you say to yourself when you became aware of the criticism? Did you say, "I am not appreciated"; "I never get anything right"; "I am stupid and nobody loves me"? Write down every thought that passed

through your mind and try to put them in the sequence in which they occurred.

• *Step 4:* At the end of the day, take your thought notebook and review all of your entries for that day. Compare them with previous entries. What do they tell you? Examine the reality of what you feel. Reinforce how irrational some of your ideas are, and how unnecessary many of your negative feelings are. Then go to exercise 1 and create a pleasant thought to end your day.

EXERCISE 5

Purpose: To identify the thoughts preceding a bothersome or ruminating thought.

• *Step 1:* When you realize that you are thinking excessively about some idea or event, stop and write down the idea in a brief sentence that completely catches the thought. Ruminating is like "chewing the cud." The thought goes round and round in your head until you feel quite dizzy. It is likely to keep you awake at night, so this exercise is helpful when you suffer from insomnia. Keep your notebook next to your bed.

• *Step 2:* Ask yourself: *"When* did this idea start?" Try to pinpoint the event or thought that began it. Perhaps it was a telephone conversation, a letter, or a visit. Briefly describe the event in your notebook.

• *Step 3:* Then ask yourself: *"Why* does this idea bother me?" The assumption is that if you have a thought going round and round in your head, it must be something that gets to you. Does it threaten you? Anger you? Aggravate you? Interfere with your wishes? Cause you to lose control? Write down a brief statement about why you think the idea troubles you.

One word of *caution:* Sometimes, especially when we are fatigued, ideas will become repetitive and ruminative when there is *no* real threat in them at all. This is caused by our tired brains and is due, in all probability, to a temporary imbalance in our brain chemistry. We often speak of being overtired and therefore unable to go to sleep. Pay no attention to your thoughts when you are this way. They are not legitimate thoughts. The problem will go away when you have had adequate sleep and when you are rested. If it persists, you need professional help.

Variation: Keep a record of all the thoughts that bother you, no matter how long they last. At the end of a week, review these thoughts and see whether there are any *themes* that keep occurring. Do certain people always bother you? Are there certain times of the day when you are more bothered than at other times? Does a particular incident always spark a reaction? By carefully recording and reviewing your reactions over a period of time, you develop considerable insight into your life environment and your own personality style. It will help you to pinpoint, very quickly, where and what you need to change.

2. THOUGHT EVALUATION

Now that you can capture the stream of your thought, the next step is to "evaluate" your thoughts. This prepares the way for change.

Whether we like it or not, we are constantly evaluating what goes on around and within us. Unfortunately, although we are not very aware of this, our emotions are largely determined by this evaluation process. Quite unconsciously we ask ourselves many questions such as: "What did he mean when he said that?" Or, "Why is she rubbing her nose that way—did I do something wrong?" Or, "I know he doesn't believe me—what am I to do?"

We interpret the thoughts, feelings, and moods of others through their words, tones, inflections, body movements, and facial expressions. We seldom accept things at face value. Our mind seems to be suspicious and distrustful by nature and all this goes on without any deliberate intention on our part.

Jesus knew that people do this. Do you remember when he healed the palsied man, with the scribes standing nearby? We read in Matthew 9:4, "And Jesus knowing their thoughts said, Wherefore think ye evil in your hearts?"

Jesus wanted people to know what they were thinking and why they were thinking it. How else could He draw attention to hypocrisy and disbelief?

By keeping ourselves alert to what is going on in our minds and by being curious and observant about our thinking, we can avoid the blind spots that characterize unsuccessful people. To know what you are thinking and why you are thinking it is to "know yourself," and to enlarge the scope of your life by making yourself open to the richness of all the wisdom of God. You are more "in tune" with God if you are more "in tune" with yourself. Thought evaluating is a simple exercise whereby the thoughts you have captured are carefully reviewed and analyzed to determine the following:

- Are they the real issue?
- Are they based on reality?
- Where are they likely to lead to now?

EXERCISE 6

Purpose: To carefully analyze a thought and determine whether there is a reason for it or not and whether the emotion following it is justified.

- *Step 1:* For this exercise you will need some 3" x 5" or similar cards or a notebook that can easily be carried with you. Prepare a number of cards (or pages in your thought notebook) as follows:

Thought:
Underlying issues:
Reasons:
Evidence:
Decision:

- *Step 2:* Take a thought you have identified or captured in the preceding exercise and write it in next to "Thought" on your card. You may wish to work on three or four thoughts at one time but don't attempt more than this. Write each thought on a different page. Try to focus on the most troublesome of your thoughts first. The more troublesome the thought, the fewer you should try to work on at one time.

- *Step 3:* You will need some thinking time for this step. Go where you cannot be disturbed and prayerfully take each of the thoughts you have written down and consider the following:

Ask yourself: "What is the *real issue* behind this thought? Is this really what is bothering me or is there a deeper issue?" Ponder your answers for a while before writing anything down. Think about the sequence of events or thoughts leading up to this troublesome thought.

Ask yourself: "What is the *underlying need* that prompts me to have a problem with this thought? Do I need love? Power? Security? Respect? Reassurance? Am I resisting change? Am I scared? Am I anxious? Is it that I just need an outlet for my feelings?"

When you feel you have developed a good understanding of the issues behind your thought, write them down, as briefly as you can, next to "Underlying issues."

- *Step 4:* Then ask yourself: "Is this issue based on *reality?* Or is it imagined?" Is it a distortion of reality? Be absolutely honest, even if you don't feel like agreeing with yourself. Write down your response next to "Reasons" on your card.

- *Step 5:* Ask yourself: "What is the *evidence* for my thought?" "Where do I get this idea from?" "What proof can I give that this is true?"

For example, let us suppose you have just been criticized by a friend for not doing him a favor. You feel depressed because of the implied rejection in your friend's comments. As you examine your thoughts, you identify one main theme: "I am a no-good worthless person unless I can please my friends at all times." The underlying issue behind this thought is your general feeling of low self-esteem and your need always to be winning the approval of others by pleasing them.

You then ask yourself: "What is the *evidence* I have that if I please others and do what they want me to do, I will be a better person?" As you ponder this question it should become obvious to you that there is *no* evidence that you will be a better person. Pleasing others only sets you up for more rejection because if you do not go on pleasing them they will be even more upset. If you please them sometimes, they will expect you to please them always. So write down on your card: "There is *no* evidence to prove that I am a better person just because I do what others expect me to do. My self-worth is not determined by pleasing others but by God's unconditional acceptance of me."

• *Step 6:* Ask yourself: "What *decision* should I therefore make? Do I decide to accept the thought and put up with the associated feeling of unworthiness, or do I reject it?"

In our example, the decision should be: "I will not allow the rejection of others (when I don't please them) to determine how I value myself. I am a worthwhile person, whether others value me or not, because God values me."

• *Step 7:* Having concluded the evaluation of your thought, keep the card in an easily accessible place. Several times each day, take out the card and review the response given to each question. Affirm yourself for these responses. Say to yourself: "I *believe* this to be true. God, help me to live my life as if it *were* true."

Variation: This exercise can also be carried out with the help of a trusted friend or as a small-group exercise. Each person identifies a thought and evaluates it as I have shown. The responses are then shared with another person or with the group, who are asked to agree or disagree with the response. The discussion should then both clarify thinking and drive home the truthfulness of conclusions. The card is then used for review and for periodically affirming yourself.

3.   THOUGHT CHALLENGING

Having captured and evaluated a thought, the third step is that of "challenging" or disputing the thought. This step is particularly important when a thought resists rational analysis or when the evidence for the thought is ambiguous.

For instance, let us suppose you are late for a dinner engagement and your host has criticized you for "always being late." You may very well have been late because you dilly-dallied while dressing or because you stopped to visit an old friend. In other words, you *are* guilty for being late. You failed to keep a promise for reasons you could have avoided. So you apologize. Your host accepts your apology. But you continue to feel guilty. You don't like yourself for being inconsiderate. You've done this many times before, and you fear that this tendency may be deeply ingrained in your personality. No one else is blaming you. Nobody else is punishing you for your error. You are doing it to yourself. What do you do now? The next exercise should help you.

EXERCISE 7

Purpose: To remove the incapacitating consequences of a particular thought by challenging the underlying beliefs or assumptions of the thought.

• *Step 1:* Select a thought that is bothering you. If you are upset, but do not know why, use exercise 4 to work backward to identify the thoughts that led up to your feeling. Let us say that the thought goes something like this:

"I should feel guilty if I do not do what others expect me to do."

This is a very common thought, especially if you are accustomed to being a victim.

• *Step 2:* Ask yourself: "Is this thought rational or irrational?" By rational, I mean is there a valid *reason* for the thought? Are you *really* guilty or do you just *feel* guilty? If you are in doubt, call the idea irrational and proceed with the next step. Labeling your thought as irrational when it *is* irrational helps to drive home the point that reality is being distorted and truth hidden.

If you can honestly say that the idea is rational, sensible, and quite logical, then give yourself permission to experience whatever you are feeling. Feeling guilty when you are guilty is necessary and normal. Feeling guilty when you are not guilty is stupid!

In the example above, we must label the thought as irrational. It does not make sense that one should feel guilty when you don't do what others expect you to do. If the thought was "I have made an error and harmed someone, therefore I feel guilty," this would be a rational statement.

Feelings that follow rational thoughts are necessary and appropriate. If you are guilty of something, then let yourself feel guilty. Accept the guilt as normal. Just make sure that you feel an appropriate amount of guilt and that it does not last too long.

How long should you feel guilty? Only long enough to seek forgiveness from the one you have harmed and from God. This may involve making reparation. Once you have received forgiveness, the feeling of guilt has served its purpose and should be disposed of quickly. If you continue feeling guilty, you are perpetuating the feeling through inappropriate self-talk.

• *Step 3:* If the thought is irrational, then proceed to challenge the thought. *Challenging* is a way of conversing with yourself in such a way that you bring into question the truthfulness (or reality) of the thought. Some psychologists call it "disputing" and see it as a way of changing the underlying beliefs that cause the thought. You fight unreality with reason. You force yourself to ask, "Is this reality?" God has given us reasoning power for this purpose.

The best way to challenge your irrational thoughts is to do it in writing. Take a thought and write it at the top of a sheet of paper. Divide the paper into two halves down the center. On the left side enter reasons why the thought is true. On the right, enter the reasons why it is not.

The following questions may help you:

- Who says it must be so?
- Is there a law that says this?
- Why should I believe this?
- Is this a hangover from childish reasoning?
- What is the worst consequence I can expect even if this were true?
- What prevents me from changing this belief?
- Are there ways I can prove or disprove this thought?
- If I take the idea to its extreme, what does it then say?

Write down all your answers and reinforce the points you are making to yourself. Debate with yourself as if you were a lawyer. Convince yourself that you can change your irrational ideas if you insist on getting at the truth in your thinking. Trust God to give you His Holy Spirit to convince you of the truth.

Variation: This exercise can also be carried out in dialogue with another, or it can be used as a small-group exercise where each member of the group is given an opportunity to work through the challenging of a thought.

4.   THOUGHT CHANGING

Changing a thought can be accomplished in one of three ways. The first method is to repeat to yourself, as often as possible, the new thought you want to replace the old. For instance, you can

write the new thought on a card. Every hour, take it out and repeat the thought to yourself. Slowly you will come to believe it.
Repetition in self-talk will change your thoughts. It works when
we say negative things to ourself all the time, so there is no reason why it shouldn't work when we say positive things.

The second method is simply to *decide* what it is you want to
believe, and believe it! This is not as hard as it may seem. If the
previous exercise of challenging an irrational belief is effective,
you should be so convinced that you change your belief without
any further ado. I've watched many of my patients do this. I've
done it many times myself. When you are convinced, you change
your mind.

It works with habits also. When we see and really believe that
sin is self-destructive we simply decide to change our behavior—
and we do!

But not everyone finds it this easy. If you cannot easily change
your thought, no matter how overwhelming the evidence for the
change is, then I suggest you see a counselor or psychotherapist.
Your thought patterns may be too deeply ingrained to respond to
self-help. This is particularly important if the thought pattern
was formed during your early-childhood period. You will not be
able to use reason, evidence, or facts to change your beliefs that
easily.

5. THOUGHT PREVENTING

Just as the body can be exercised to increase its resistance to
disease, so can the mind be exercised to increase its resistance to
unpleasant thoughts or emotions. Prevention is better than cure.
This is as true in the realm of our emotions as it is in our bodies.

Rather than waiting for an emotional or thought problem to
arise, you can rehearse your reality thinking during your sane
moments.

The creative reader could, no doubt, think of a number of
ways to do this. Rather than by spelling out step-by-step instruc-

tions for a specific exercise, I will outline some general principles and leave the reader to be creative.

EXERCISE 8

Purpose: To teach oneself to think more rationally during times of normal emotion, and to practice healthy thinking.

Action: Prepare a list of your unique and commonly used irrational ideas. You can use the list I give at the end of this chapter as a starting point and add as many others as you wish. Play a game with yourself. See how many rational counter-statements you can devise for each irrational thought. Write your personalized responses on cards and keep them with you for frequent reviewing. Use Scripture wherever you can, to support your rational counter-statements. This will help you to develop the habit of raional thinking so that it can be used spontaneously when a real-life situation occurs.

Variation: You could set up a system whereby you reward yourself for each new rational counter-thought or argument you create. Give points for each idea, and treat yourself to some minor luxury when you have reached a predetermined goal.

EXERCISE 9

Purpose: Teaching yourself new "mind games" to improve your rational thinking.

Action: We learn many negative and self-destructive mind-games in life, but few positive. Negative mind-games are patterns of fixed responses to situations in which the "rules" are predetermined, well rehearsed, and continue indefinitely unless you do something to stop them. In this exercise I will describe a series of negative mind-games and then suggest positive alternatives. You may be able to design some positive mind-games that fit your personal needs. Try your hand at this. You may be surprised at how creative you can be.

(a) A common negative mind-game is saying the most ridiculous things to yourself and not realizing how ridiculous they are! What you say to yourself determines your feelings and behavior. If you are being irritated, say, by a neighbor's barking dog, as I was recently, don't say to yourself, "I can't stand it! That noise is driving me crazy." Saying this to yourself doesn't remove the irritation, it merely prescribes how you are going to feel.

The truth is that you *can* stand it, and it will *not* drive you crazy. Learn to speak the *truth* to yourself. An alternative is to say, "That dog's barking is very irritating to me. I will call the neighbor and ask him to take care of the dog." Such a self-statement brings change. It specifies the action that is to be taken. Similarly, don't say to yourself, "I can't do it," or "Things should be better," or "This is going to hurt me." These self-statements become self-fulfilling prophecies. Learn to recognize them and substitute healthier and more truthful alternatives.

(b) Watch the derogatory labels you use on yourself. Another common negative mind-game is convincing yourself that you are humble by labeling yourself in a derogatory way. "Oh, I suppose I'm just stupid," or "I'm just paranoid, don't pay attention to me." These labels are *defense mechanisms*. You're afraid others will think this way of you, so you jump in first to avoid the pain of finding out what they think.

Again, these become self-fulfilling prophecies. They are not honest and they distort reality. Always label your feelings correctly. Don't say, "I am stupid," but rather "I'm sorry, I made a mistake, I will try to do better next time." Don't say, "I am paranoid (schizophrenic, hole-in-my-head, getting old and senile, or any other derogatory label)." Say, "I tend to worry easily," or "I'm not looking at things realistically." A healthy self-attitude can never exist if you label yourself in a derogatory manner.

(c) Another common negative mind-game is to agree with the names others call you. If they say, "You're stupid," you agree as a way of avoiding further conflict. Do not do this. Receive the label with gracious repudiation. Refuse to accept the general descriptions others place on you. If a spouse says, "You always do this to me," remind him that *always* means "every time" and there must be at least one exception to this rule in your behavior. There are two important things to remember about name-calling: The first is that it is used as a weapon to punish others; the second is that words are only symbols.

Words are only symbols, yet we irrationally and unrealistically respond to them as if they were real in themselves. Words are used to punish others. Gone are the days when we could pull out a six-shooter and take care of our enemy. Now we use verbal six-shooters, full of choice and well-chosen derogatory labels, dipped in the poison of our rage and sharpened by all the "inside knowledge" we have on a person's vulnerable and tender spots. But the bullets are only words. They can be dodged by simply removing their symbolic meaning and remembering that they are only designed to punish us.

Jesus has taken all the questionable fun out of revenge! Gone is the superficial pleasure of seeing others cringe at our venomous labels. In its place He has given us some simple rules:

> But I say unto you, Love your enemies, bless them
> that curse you, do good to them that hate you, and
> pray for them which despitefully use you, and perse-
> cute you; That ye may be the children of your Father
> which is in heaven . . . (Matthew 5:44–45).

This is a better reality than hatred.

Irrational and Rational Thoughts

Drawing on the ideas of a number of other writers (including Albert Ellis) I have compiled some examples of irrational and rational counterpoints of the same thought, as I see them. Study these carefully so as to get a good feel for the difference between the two. Then compile a list of your own unique irrational thoughts and work out some healthy, rational alternatives.

Irrational Thought	*Rational Thought*
1. Everybody must love me at all times, no matter what I do.	People respond to love with love. If I expect love, I must give love.
2. I am only a worthy person if I do what others expect of me.	My self-worth is not dependent on the acceptance of others. I am therefore free to choose my own actions.
3. I must never experience any emotional pain.	Life is full of potential for emotional pain. I must learn to deal with it to the best of my ability.
4. Things should always turn out the way I expect them to.	There is no law that says my expectations should always be fulfilled. I must, at all times, only expect what realistically can be achieved.
5. My happiness is dependent on others doing what pleases me, or giving me the respect I crave.	My happiness is determined by my own actions and attitudes and not by others.
6. If I make one mistake, then this cancels my previous successes.	One mistake (or two, or three) does not make a catastrophe. I cannot expect myself to be so perfect as never to make a mistake.
7. Because others expect me to be perfect, I must continue and strive at all costs to live up to their expectations.	I am only human, and therefore I am imperfect. It is unreasonable for others to expect me to so distort my life as to live up to their expectations.
8. Because I am good at some things, I expect myself to be good at all things.	Every person has his or her limits. I must accept my limitations and make the most of my strengths.

Irrational Thought	*Rational Thought*
9. No one must dislike me. I must dislike no one.	I cannot expect everyone to like me. I am called to love others, not necessarily like them. Christ loved the unlikable.
10. I can be extremely happy without doing anything to achieve it.	Happiness is not automatic. It is achieved by hard work, dedication to God's purposes, and the grace to accept failure as the means of growth.
11. The reason I am all messed up emotionally is that my parents didn't do a good job of parenting.	I must not blame others for what I am. I am quite capable of changing if I don't like who I have become.
12. There are many things in life that make me unhappy, and I have no control over them.	My happiness is a choice. Most things that happen in life are controllable. I must learn to overcome my tendency toward helplessness.
13. I must never feel down or depressed. If I do, I am a failure.	Much depression is a natural response to loss. I can neither avoid it nor should I. I must learn how to accept loss as a natural consequence of living.
14. It is easier to avoid than face life's difficulties. If I avoid the fearful or unpleasant, it will go away.	If something is unpleasant or fearsome, I can best deal with it by facing it courageously and changing what I can.
15. I have no control over how other people or events make me feel. I am the victim of forces outside me.	I cannot blame others for my feelings. I can control my emotions if I choose to work at changing my thinking, beliefs, and attitudes.
16. If someone else does something better than I do, I am inferior to that person.	I must give others permission to be better than I am without feeling resentment or envy. I am not a god.

Irrational Thought	*Rational Thought*
17. If I make a decision, I must have no lingering doubts. At all times I should be positive and unwavering.	To doubt is to be human. Very few decisions have an absolute right or wrong. I accept my doubt as part of my imperfection.
18. Strong people never ask others for help. If I show anyone that I am not perfectly strong, they won't trust me.	The greatest sign of strength is to know your limitations. People trust people who are honest about themselves, not those who try to prove they are superhuman.
19. It is my mission in life to put everyone else right, to fight all injustice (as I see it), and to punish all wrongdoing in others.	"Jesus saith unto him, [Peter]. . . . what is that to thee? follow thou me" (John 21:22). God is the final judge of all human actions. God does the punishing around here, not me. Let me take care that in judging others, I don't condemn myself.
20. If something seems dangerous or awful, I must continually think and worry about it because it will then come out right.	Anxiety does not change anything. It does not clothe lilies nor take care of the morrow. By faith, I cast my cares on Jesus because He cares for me, and by faith I will leave them there.

Changing Your Self-Feelings

Chapter 11

Our culture believes two things about people, that have important implications. First, it believes that all people are highly malleable. Anyone can become anything he or she wants to become. This is a myth that creates a ready and lucrative market for certain diets, new therapies, jogging, aerobics, and a host of other fads. More money is made capitalizing on the idea that people can change for the better, than on any other.

Second, it believes that everyone should have high self-esteem. But how high is enough? And where does humility fit into the picture? Let us see how reality thinking can help us feel better about ourselves without violating basic Christian principles.

Can We Change?

The need to alter ourselves has reached epidemic proportions. As Bernie Zilbergeld points out in his book *The Shrinking of America*, there are three key assumptions of our present age that feed this. The first is that human beings *should* change because

171

they are not as competent or as good or as happy as they could be. The second is that there are *few* limits to the alternatives they can make for themselves. The third is that change is relatively *easy* to effect. All you need is the right method and attitude and you can become almost whatever you want to become.

True? I doubt it. And I am in the business of helping people to change! Oh, I believe that people can be happier, more fulfilled, and achieve greater successes, but it takes a lot more than what most success peddlers have to sell. It takes hard, body-aching, mind-wrenching, soul-searching work. Even to just be happy! This is the reality by which we must live.

Unfortunately, most people seeking change want it to happen without hard work. They want "instant improvements—with a money back guarantee!" They want to lose weight while still eating as much as their stomachs will hold, so they take "starch blocking" pills. The surplus food is supposed to pass right through you without pausing for as much as a "howdy." They want to exercise without moving a muscle, so they go to spas that use "electrostimulators" to activate and use muscles while they lie still on a couch. They want a suntan without going into the sun, so they take tanning pills. I don't know of any way of achieving a successful life that doesn't require effort. There are no instant "success pills."

False Gods

As a psychologist, I am very aware of how easily psychology can become a substitute for religion. Many systems of psychotherapy become altars to be worshiped at. In times past the Bible was always the common reference point and converts were the ones claiming miracles. Today secular people claim miracles as well: through EST, primal screaming, meditation, and nude swimming! We can so easily set up false gods.

The reason for their success is not that these life- and personality-changing systems are so effective. Most times they are not. It's just that people will believe almost anything if given a plausible

reason. They will change behavior, feelings, tendencies to helplessness, and even their programming for success or failure if
they can be made to change their beliefs about themselves and
therefore their thinking. Most humans are extremely gullible and
easily influenced for good or evil.

I believe that most people are basically healthy and resource-
ful. There is a resiliency that allows them to bounce back from
most apparent catastrophes, pick up the pieces, and reconstruct a
meaningful life. Some need counseling and psychotherapy. They
are handicapped by past traumatic events, faulty rearing by parents, bad habits, or disturbed body chemistry. They must learn
how to overcome these handicaps. No amount of praying is
going to take away problems we create for ourselves. *We* must
change. God does not always work miracles that bypass our basic
psychology or our need to grow. He is in the refining business—
this is reality. He does not always circumvent our responsibility
for what we must do for ourselves.

Where Is Help?

For people needing to change, Christian psychological help is
hardly a false god. It is the handmaiden of the Gospel, helping
many to sweep out the cobwebs of lethargy and clear away the
grime and slime of ineffectiveness and self-destruction so that the
Gospel can be more fully appropriated. This why I am in the
business of Christian psychotherapy.

Where many make their mistake is in believing that a great
reservoir of unused power lies solely within them. This is what is
promised by so many modern therapies and positive thinkers.
"You can have high self-esteem if you believe in yourself," they
say. If I could believe in myself, I wouldn't need high self-esteem! The power is *not* within us. It comes from without, from
releasing God in our lives. This is a better reality: I can become
anything God wants me to become because He can give me the
power to become it.

God's power is a reality for me, as it is for all Christians. I know it from personal experience. It is available to heal, help, change, subdue, save, and keep me from falling. It is available to all believers. It is a far greater power than the best I can muster from within myself. But don't make the mistake of thinking it can make you into anything you choose.

Hindrances to God's Power

Unfortunately, what I am as a person can be a major obstacle to the power of God in my life. It does not have to be an obstacle since God is able to do anything He wants to, but reality is that God will not perpetuate my lack of full and complete commitment to Him. He is a wise God. He knows me through and through. And while He provides us with the resources to change, He will not do for us what we must do for ourselves. He does what we can't do for ourselves.

Do you remember when Jesus came to Nazareth, His "own country," and taught in the synagogue? The people asked, "Is not this the carpenter's son? Is he not just one of us? His sisters are still here. Wasn't his mother Mary?" (*see* Matthew 13:55,56). Then we are told, "And he [Jesus] did not many mighty works there because of their unbelief" (Matthew 13:58).

Jesus was hindered from doing His work of miracles by the beliefs and attitudes of the people of Nazareth. It is not that He could not perform miracles there, but that He would not. God's grace may be free, but it is not cheap. I believe that we can similarly hinder the work of Christ in our lives.

What are some of the ways I can hinder God's work in me? Here are a few:

- I don't believe that God's power is available to me.
- I don't believe that God has any power to give me.
- I don't believe I deserve to have God's power available to me.
- I am afraid of the consequences of having God's power in me.

• I am too impatient to wait for God's power to work in me.

• I cannot abandon myself to God since I cannot trust anyone.

These are just some of the ways we can shut off God's power. They are psychological handicaps. They are "belief barriers." We have learned them through faulty child rearing, distorted preaching, or unfortunate life circumstances.

There are also natural encumbrances that can shut us off from God's power. Hebrews 12:1 talks of "weights" as well as "sins" that can prevent us from "running with patience the race that is set before us." We don't "look to Jesus," because our faith eyes are crusted over with personal hurt, faulty ways of behaving, and muddled thinking patterns.

If we think realistically, we can learn how to remove these hindrances and thus free God's power in and through us.

Who Am I?

You cannot change or feel better about yourself if you don't really know who you are. You cannot become what God wants you to be if you don't know yourself.

Unfortunately the expression "knowing who you are" has become somewhat of a hackneyed cliché, but it is nevertheless an important starting point in all self-growth. The truth of the matter is that every human being possesses the capacity to reflect upon herself or himself and form an understanding of who they are. This is what is called self-consciousness. Out of it there develops a self-image, which is literally a picture of the self stored in the memory and which defines who and what you are. It is the sum total of *all* you believe about yourself.

If you take a moment, you can write down a description of yourself that captures this self-image. Divide a sheet of paper into two halves. On the left side place the heading "my good points" and on the right place "my bad points." Now start writing. Be honest and courageous. Even if you are not sure about a characteristic or trait, write it down! Use a second sheet of paper if you must, but set down *everything* about yourself before you go any further . . . I will wait for you! . . . Review the list again. Are you sure you've got it all? Do not be afraid to look honestly at yourself.

Do you remember the story of Narcissus? He was a beautiful Greek shepherd boy who was loved by a young girl named Echo. When he failed to love her in return, she pined away and died. Nemesis, the goddess of retribution, forced Narcissus to gaze into a stream. Immediately he fell so in love with his own reflection that he fell into the water and drowned. Some say he was transformed into a stream flower called the narcissus, but you can't believe everything you hear!

This myth has been used by psychoanalysts to scare us away from looking too much at ourselves—especially to be less narcissistic. But there is an appropriate self-reflection we must all carry out at times.

Your Self-Esteem

Your self-image is extremely important to your psychological and spiritual health because it determines how you feel about yourself, what you believe you are capable of becoming, and whether you can trust God to do His work in you.

Most times the images we have stored in our mind about who we are, are grossly distorted. The human mind is not very reliable. It easily rearranges facts and feelings to produce the wrong effect. Despite its wonderful complexity, it can be trained to do bizarre things. It reacts to the feedback it receives from its earliest years in such an unrealistic way that very few of us reach adulthood with a clear and accurate picture of who we are. We either distort our self-image in a negative way (I am a terrible person) or in an exaggerated positive way (I am better than others). Both ways are a distortion of reality.

In our culture we tend to distort our self-image in the negative direction. In other words, most people end up not liking who they are and wishing they were someone else. Ridiculous? Yes, but true! Look at your list of good and bad points you wrote down earlier. If you have been frank, your bad points probably outnumbered your good points!

One of my students recently told me how, at age thirty, he had suddenly come to the realization that he is not the person he always believed he was. His image of himself (shaped by childhood reactions of parents and peers) was that he was fat, slow, a born loser, unlovable, unlikeable, sluggish, and only slightly intelligent. For years he carried this picture of himself in the wallet of his mind. It has shaped his life in many unfortunate ways. It sent him first pursuing a career in the ministry, where he hoped he would earn instant respect from adoring parishioners. He became a minister for the wrong reason!

After floundering for a while and not getting the respect he longed for, he finally confronted his distorted self-image in one of my classes and through therapy came to the realization that he was not the bad person he thought he was. He was not horrible, unattractive, and unlovable. After all, God loved him, so he couldn't be that bad. This truth set him free. The reality of who he truly was abolished the chains of slavery to his self-hate and self-rejection. Reality thinking demands that we develop an accurate image of ourselves so that we can know who we really are. We are then free to change what we can, or accept what we cannot.

Scripture and Low Self-Esteem

In New Testament times the tendency of people was to distort their self-image in the exaggerated positive direction. Today we tend mostly to develop negative and self-hating images. We do not, therefore, have a clear biblical teaching about low self-esteem. It seems to be a modern phenomenon.

However, to the Romans Paul had to write:

". . . do not be conceited or think too highly of yourself . . ."
(Romans 12:3 NEB).

The principle here is no different from having a negative self-image. It is still distortion, even though it exaggerates self-worth in the positive direction.

People in Paul's day tended to take too much pride in who they were. "I am a Jew" or "I am a Roman" were self-statements designed to create feelings of superiority. While we may, to some extent, be guilty of similar self-attitudes today, our culture's preoccupation with performance and success tends to create quite the opposite.

If Paul were writing to us today, I believe he would say something like this:

"Why do you always see the worst in yourself? Can't you be truthful and admit when you are good as readily as you do when you are bad?"

In either case, Paul's prescription would be the same, ". . . but think your way to a sober estimate [of yourself] based on the measure of faith that God has dealt to each of you" (Romans 12:3 NEB).

The Basis of Self-Esteem

We need to be more honest in how we feel about ourselves. We need to be willing to admit our strengths as well as our weaknesses.

If we have distorted our self-image so as to become conceited, then let us pray for the courage to come "down" to reality. If we have rejected ourselves because we believe we are useless, hopeless and unlovable, then let us pray for the courage to come "up" to reality. We need to be sober in all our self-judgments. The art of being yourself is letting God determine your self-image. Let Him be the mirror of your true self—and then glory in what He shows you to be.

How Does Low Self-Esteem Damage Us?

Low self-esteem damages us because:

1. It blocks out God's full power in our life. If we do not respect ourselves, we will not let God have us fully. While we always feel "unworthy" of God's love, we must never feel "worthless" within ourselves. There is an important difference between feeling that you have not earned God's forgiveness (grace) and the neurotic groveling of worthlessness that cannot even receive God's forgiveness.

2. It blocks our awareness of alternative actions. We say to ourselves, "I cannot make it. I am no good. I will never be able to accomplish anything." We adopt the attitude of "why bother?"

3. It distorts our expectations of ourselves. We may exceed reality in our attempt to compensate, or we may aim too low.

4. We become hostile. We are angry because we feel we are no good—and this sets us up for battle. We blame, criticize, and condemn.

5. We demand unreasonable expectations for others— which they cannot fulfill. "See," we often say to ourselves, "you cannot trust anyone."

6. It sets up future failure by viewing past failure as an unalterable pattern. "If I have failed once, I will fail always" is the belief.

How Do We Create Low Self-Esteem?

The reasons are many and complex. All I know is that ultimately it is a way of *thinking*. The solution must therefore be found in changing this way of thinking.

All our thinking about ourselves is shaped by our early home environment, parental attitudes, peer reactions, and our individ-

ual personality characteristics. By and large it is created by someone's setting up standards we cannot live up to. Later, we inter-
nalize these standards and still cannot live up to them. We are always "falling short." We cannot outrun, outplay, outwit,
outperform, outlook, or outsatisfy some arbitrary standard we
have set up in our imagination, usually to please someone else. It
is a lost cause, so we are bound to feel inadequate.

Sometimes, distorted self-images are caused by cruel and cal-
lous parents. They label their children as "useless," "hopeless,"
and "evil." They think they are motivating them to do better.
This child is supposed to rise up in response to the challenge and
try to overcome the label by being a better person. It usually fails
to accomplish this and leaves the child feeling bad. One father
actually admitted to me that he told his twelve-year-old son at
least once a day that he would never amount to anything, because he believed that this would serve as an incentive to the boy.
His son, he hoped, would rise up and prove to the father that he
could amount to something. Unfortunately, his son believed his
dad and is now a dropout and drug addict.

If you are guilty of such distorted psychology, then correct it
right away. Children believe what you tell them, not what you
intend to communicate. You can't tell a child "I hate you" and
then expect him to believe that you love him just because you
take him fishing or to a baseball game. If you try to shame a child
into new behavior, you will only create feelings of shame. These
could last a lifetime.

How Do We Perpetuate Low Self-Esteem?

While these are some ways in which we create distorted self-
images, they don't explain how *or why* we perpetuate them. Most
of us become adults who feel terrible about ourselves with no
clear self-image or, at least, with one that we hate. But need we
forever be handicapped by it? Must it continue to control our
feelings, behavior, successes, or failures, day in and day out?

Obviously not! We can change our thinking and take control of our distorted self-image.

Let me suggest a few ways in which we perpetuate our self-images in the hope that you will recognize your style.

1. Some don't know they have a distorted self-image, so they perpetuate it out of *ignorance.*

I frequently encounter people who were overweight when they were young. Later they become thin but continue to think of themselves as fat. One minister, attending a class I was teaching, shared how he always thought of himself as shy and timid. In social settings he felt terrible because he could not relate in an open way. I told him that he was quite assertive, open, and not a bit shy. He was surprised and a little disbelieving. The other ministers in the class quickly confirmed my observation. Slowly he was convinced to change his self-perception. He admitted he had changed over the years in his behavior yet retained a distorted self-image.

If you suspect that you do this, perform the following exercise:

a) Take the "good and bad points" work sheet you prepared earlier. Review your list again and make sure it adequately reflects what you believe about yourself.

For example, do you believe you are handsome or attractive? Unattractive? Friendly? Withdrawn? Overly defensive? Focus on your image of yourself.

b) Ask a spouse or close friend to go over this list with you and *honestly* tell you whether your description is accurate or not. Be courageous. Receive the feedback with all the honesty you can muster. If you disagree with the feedback, then ask a second friend to arbitrate.

c) Then correct your list. Delete those characteristics that are not true and modify the self-statements for those that are partly true. Ask your spouse or friend whether they agree with the new list. If not, correct it again.

d) Then pray for help to adjust your self-image to conform to this reality.

One caution: If your spouse or friend has reason to be angry with you, then don't trust the feedback. An exercise like this can be very destructive in the hands of someone who has reason to punish you.

2.   Some perpetuate a distorted self-image through the belief that they cannot change anything. They fail to act because of *helplessness*. To be helpless is to believe that nothing you do makes any difference. It is an attitude of your mind—an immobilization that begins in your thoughts and nowhere else.

The phenomenon of helplessness has been demonstrated through a fascinating experiment using dogs. The experiment proves how powerful our beliefs are to immobilize us. In the experiment, two groups of dogs are placed in a room with a cage. The cage is constructed so that shocks can be administered through the floor to the dog's paws. The top of the cage is removable, so that in the one situation it is left in place and the dog cannot escape. In the second situation it can be removed and the dog is free to jump out of the cage.

With the top in place, dogs from the first group are placed in the cage, one at a time, and shocks applied to the paws. At first, the dogs panic, jump around, and try to find a way out. Since the top is in place they are trapped. After a while they accept the shocks as inevitable and passively sink to the cage floor, receiving all the discomfort, and making no further attempt to escape.

With the second group of dogs, the same procedure is followed, except the top of the cage is removed. These dogs quickly learn that they can escape the shocks by jumping out of the cage.

Now when these two groups of dogs are taken to a second room where a similar cage (but without a top) is set up, a strange phenomenon is observed. The second group, trained with the top off, quickly escape from the shocks. The first group, trained with the top in place, passively settle to the floor to receive the shocks with little resistance. They believe there is no escape! This phenomenon has been called *learned helplessness*. It has also been demonstrated in many other experiments using humans.

Helplessness is all around us. It explains why so many persons continue to experience painful life situations and make little effort to escape or change anything. It accounts for why many are the victims of wife beating, child abuse, rape, crime, and so on. Learned helplessness, taught through many childhood and early-adult experiences, convinces people that they are unable to do anything about what is happening to them. They believe they have no power, and this belief prevents them from taking action or changing their circumstances. This belief also creates low self-esteem.

In many subtle and less obvious areas of psychological functioning, helplessness can immobilize you. Because your father called you "stupid" when you were a child, you continue to behave as if you are stupid. Because an ex-spouse says you are "selfish and beastly," you continue to behave selfishly and beastly. You behave what you believe! But you don't have to believe it if it isn't true.

The solution to all forms of helplessness is quite simple: *Change your beliefs!*

Stop thinking that what you believe is true. Challenge the validity of your erroneous self-image and open yourself to new possibilities. Look up! The top of the cage is *off*. Look around you. You are a free person. With God on your side, *all things are possible!* God is not a God of helplessness or fear, but a God of infinite possibilities. *This is reality!* Risk believing it!

The Damaging Consequences of Distorted Self-Image

If you have a distorted picture of yourself stored in your memory, the damaging consequences are painful and many.

• You will not have self-esteem but self-hate. All through life you will find fault with, and keep rejecting, yourself. Never will you know the full joy of God's love. You'll hate yourself too much to be able to receive it freely and unconditionally.

• You will constantly want to hurt or punish yourself.

Self-punishment takes many subtle forms, but it is ultimately a usurping of the cross. If you punish yourself, you rob the cross of its power to give you the forgiveness you so desperately need.

• You will not be able to build deep, abiding friendships. You are not at peace with yourself; how can you be at peace with others? If you don't love yourself, how can you love others? Shakespeare wrote, "To thine own self be true, and it must follow, as the night day, thou canst not then be false to any man."

• You will not be able to nurture others or be nurtured by them. Intimacy will be difficult because people with distorted self-images must hide from themselves and others behind a facade. No one must know who you really are! So you keep plenty of distance between you and them.

• You will not be able to forgive yourself. You will always believe that you deserve what happens to you. Failure will be a poison and not a power—an anchor that drags you down rather than wings that can help you to soar.

• You will not know what it is to be a *real* person. You will feel like a phony! Self-images of hypocrisy will haunt you. You feel that there's really two of you: the person others see, and the person you believe you are.

Whatever else it means to be a *real* and mature person, there is general agreement among many psychologists that this is a person with a high degree of internal unity. There is coherence and congruence. What you are on the outside is what you are on the inside. Jesus was such a person! We are called and given the power to be such persons also.

How Do We Build Self-Esteem?

I have shown that low self-esteem is the consequence of having a negative self-image. If you believe you are "crummy," don't be surprised if you feel crummy about yourself. Your first task, therefore, has been to correct any distortion you may have in your mental picture of yourself.

Most often this picture is negative. Once you have disposed of the distorted elements, you will be left with some things about yourself that you don't like. What do you do with these? You can do two things: (1) You can change what you don't like; and (2) you can accept what you cannot change.

Complete self-acceptance, based on realistic self-knowledge, is what creates a healthy self-esteem. It does not come from accomplishing great feats or being successful, although these can help you to become more self-accepting.

The most beautiful people I know are not pretty or handsome, necessarily. Their beauty is from within and it radiates everywhere. It shines in a dark and unhappy world. It helps them to weather the most cruel of life's storms.

What is this beauty? Where does it come from? I believe it is the end product of this simple principle: *They don't want to change anything about themselves.*

They love themselves *as they are.* Their self-love is totally unconditional. They can look you in the face, fairly and squarely, and say, "Here I am. This is all there is of me. God loves it. I love it. You can love it also if you choose."

I love these people. I trust I am becoming more and more like this myself. They have embraced reality and are content with it.

Are there some practical steps that can move us toward this complete self-acceptance? Yes, here are a few:

1.   *Stop degrading yourself—inwardly or outwardly.* This is a habit for many of us and it undermines self-acceptance. It is neurotic·and unnecessary. Humility is *not* putting yourself down or denying your talents. Humility is making sure you don't put yourself above others. Whenever you catch yourself putting yourself down, *stop!* Don't go any further. Say to yourself, "I have no right to degrade myself." Then look more realistically at what you are doing.

2.   *Use positive reinforcement statements* (PRS). These are statements made in favor of yourself. You can affirm what you want to become, or something you have just done, by saying to

yourself or someone else, "I did a great job." This is *not* the same
as pride. If you are positive toward yourself, others will be also.
Here are some examples:

You've just completed a project on time for your boss. He fails
to mention it. Say to yourself:

"Hey, I really worked hard to complete that job. I thank
God He gives me the strength to do it."

This is better than saying:

"What a crummy boss. I hate him for not thanking me."

You've just cooked a great meal and entertained your spouse's
parents. They have been a little critical and unappreciative. Say
to yourself:

"I am a good hostess. God has given me a great gift. I am
glad I can be successful with the gifts God has given me."

These PRS's can be words spoken aloud, thoughts you think,
or simply a moment of silence when you enjoy your peace. They
must be honest and realistic, otherwise they only distort reality.
Don't exaggerate your accomplishments (this is pride), just thank
God for them in a positive way. You will begin to feel better
about yourself and be more self-accepting if you do this
regularly.

3. *Learn to value your true worth.* What is our true worth?
Twenty-five cents of chemicals? Hardly. Our true worth is the
value God places on each of us. It cannot be counted in money
or weighed in gold. I know that God sees us each as infinitely
worthwhile.

But do you value yourself? You cannot go through life if you
don't, and expect to be completely self-accepting.

We *all* have both good and bad points, assets and liabilities.
Our task is to make the most of our assets while minimizing (*not*
totally eliminating) liabilities. We can accomplish this if we
value ourselves enough.

We each possess an untold capacity for reconstruction and
readaptation. Let us value this. We can all be loving, kind, patient, and helpful. Let us put a premium on this. The world

values power, prestige, good looks, strength, intelligence, and position. God hates them when they destroy us; let us not value these too much. Measure yourself, each day, by God's yardstick and actively thank Him for each evidence of your worthwhileness.

What Can You Become?

Can you become anything you want to be? Unfortunately not. Your genes, for one, will place some limits on your potential. God will have some limits also—though I find some Christians don't readily accept this. When Scripture speaks of the "body of Christ" (for example, in 1 Corinthians 12:12–31) it is clear that some of us must be content to be a toe, while others get to be the more glamorous hands or fingers.

Whatever your potential is in the precious life God has given you, it will only be glorious and radiant if it fulfills what God wants you to be. Believe this. Trust this. Follow it with all your heart.

But your problem may be of a different sort. God may want you to be an arm or a head. If so, don't be content to remain a toe. Rise up and claim your potential.

What blocks most men and women from fully developing their gifts and achieving adequate self-esteem is not their lack of talent or their inborn genetic or other limitations. It is their failure to develop and use the talents they have to the fullest. They don't respond to the call of God.

They fail to tap the depths of their richness. They bring to God the dregs of their potential and expect Him to bless it with abundance. God cooperates with those willing to bring Him their everything. He doesn't play with half-hearted commitment or lazy enthusiasm.

Don't tinker with God. He knows what He wants. Don't tinker with yourself. Using reality thinking to pursue God's plan for your life requires hard, serious, and sometimes heartbreaking work. There are no easy handouts in God's Kingdom. If you mean business with God, He will give you the power to overcome your every weakness and those obstacles you fear.

Try God and see what He can do for you! He can make you holistically successful—in every part of your being. This is my prayer for you.